DEATH WISH

You had to be willing to fight. That was what the hero always taught the sodbusters.

We have been teaching ourselves that lesson for thousands of years and we haven't learnt it yet.

He was beginning to learn it. It was what made him want to return to the dark street and find the scared kid with the knife.

I feel like a fight. So help me I feel like a fight.

But you had to use your head. Your guts said one thing, your head said another, and your guts usually won; but still you had to use your head, and the head made it crystal clear it wasn't enough to let blind rage sweep over you – because next time it wouldn't be a scared kid, next time it would be a hoodlum with a gun, and lunatic rage was no match for a gun. The only match for a gun was a gun of your own.

Death Wish

_____

Brian Garfield

CORONET BOOKS
Hodder Fawcett Ltd., London

Copyright © 1972 by Brian Garfield
First published by Hodder and
Stoughton Ltd., 1973
Coronet edition 1974

Printed and bound in Great Britain for
Coronet Books, Hodder Fawcett Ltd,
St. Paul's House, Warwick Lane,
London, EC4P 4AH
By C. Nicholls & Company Ltd,
The Philips Park Press, Manchester

ISBN 0 340 16786 6

For LARRY
and LORETTA

1

Later he worked out where he had been at the time of the attack on Esther and Carol.

It must have been a few minutes after the lunch broke up. It had been a bibulous meeting with the clients and Paul had felt the effect of the gibsons. A trifle unsteady, he had come outside with Sam Kreutzer and they had ambushed a cab at Fifty-fifth Street. Going down Seventh Avenue they had got caught in the jam in upper Times Square and Paul remembered half choking on the blurted noxious gases of a bus beside the cab. It must have happened right about then: the police placed the time of the attack at two-forty.

The middle of a torpid day. Tourists and hookers moved along the curbs empty-eyed in wilted clothing. On the corners men in sooty T-shirts sold toys and belts. Ordinarily you couldn't see the pollution working on your lungs so you ignored it; but the fumes from the bus started Paul coughing and that brought on a taut gin headache. He rubbed his eyes.

Sam Kreutzer lit up. "It's getting so you don't dare breathe anything that hasn't been filtered through a cigarette." Blew smoke at his match. "Christ will you look at that monstrosity."

"Which?"

"One Astor Plaza."

Concrete and plastic on the site of the old Astor Hotel. "I'll meet you at the Astor Bar," Sam Kreutzer said musingly, and it stirred Paul's recollection.

"A God damn shame. The politicians complain about vandalism while they're tearing down historic monuments to make room for those egg-crates."

The cab jerked forward and made half a block. Paul said, "How's the house-hunting?"

"No progress. We spent the weekend looking in Westchester."

"Maybe you ought to try looking farther out."

"I couldn't stand a long commute. But we're starting to think about renting a house – maybe Leonia or Fort Lee. Anything to get out of Manhattan. We should've done it years ago." Sam tapped his knee. "You and Esther ought to do the same thing. Why stay here when you don't have to go on living in a war zone?"

"We tried it once," Paul said and made a negative gesture with his hand, turning it over.

"Twenty years ago. Things have changed, Paul."

Above the 42nd Street roofs the sun was weak and watery through vapours, too frail to burn the eye. "You're a nut," Sam said. "You think you can tell me with a straight face you still love the city – but I'd like to hear you explain why."

"If you need to have it explained you won't understand it anyway."

"I used to know a priest who used that argument to prove the existence of God."

"Well, it made sense to the priest because he didn't need proof."

"Yeah." Very dry. Sam flashed his keyboard-length rows of teeth under the flimsy moustache he had grown on vacation and was planning, he said vaguely, to shave off. It gave him a rakish look; he was a thin slothful Minnesotan who in eight years with the firm had assimilated all the New York styles: sideburns obscured his ears, his hair fluffed out fashionably in the back, he wore flared striped suits and modish loud ties and he had learned the accepted litanies of outspoken disrespect for every Establishment value. All that, and he would never be a New Yorker. You can't take the small town out of the boy.

The cab driver was edging frantically to the left to make the left turn off Broadway into Forty-second.

"Look at this mess." Sam waved his cigarette at Times Square, the crowds, the traffic. "It just doesn't make sense any more. You can't get a guy on the phone because he's always in a taxi stuck in a traffic jam on his way to a meeting. The phone system's no good, the mails don't get through."

Sam threw his hands up helplessly; he enjoyed exposition. "The sanitation trucks grind down my street in the middle of the night like Sherman tanks with busted mufflers and they spent a Goddamned hour slamming garbage cans around right under the window. If we get a snowstorm it takes them a week to clean the streets. It's madness. Only one answer to it."

Paul smiled a little. "All right, since you obviously want me to feed you your line. What's the answer to it?"

"Only one solution to it. Abolish the environment. There won't be anything left to pollute."

Paul gave it the polite chuckle it deserved.

Sam said, "You pay for private schools for the kids. You pay for private security guards on the door. You pay out money and flesh to burglars and muggers. You write off your freedom of movement after sundown. And so on and so forth." He looked at Paul in alarm. "Christ, what am I *doing* here?"

"Making a living," Paul drawled. "And reciting the

standard of catechism of complaints just like the rest of us."

"Well, at least I'm not carrying it one step beyond that into your lunatic extreme of liberal goodness."

"What do you mean?"

"You're a Goddamned bleeding-heart, Paul, do you know that? You and Esther actually go out into the wilderness and *do* things. Look at those hideous pinholes in your lapel – what was that, your Lindsay campaign button or your Support Prison Reform badge?"

"Somebody's got to give a damn," Paul said.

2

He had been with the accounting firm of Ives, Gregson & Co. long enough to rate a window office on the Lexington Avenue side of the eighteenth floor with his name in gilt lettering on the door's frosted pane: *Paul R. Benjamin.* It was a small room with a deep carpet and push-button phone. The air-conditioner purred faintly. He settled into the chair with relief and chewed up two aspirins. Gremlins had filled his In box again but he didn't reach for it immediately. He sat absorbing comfort from the monolithic massiveness of the office and the elderly Graybar Building which contained it: there was certainty, permanence, solidity.

Thelma buzzed Bill Dundee into the office. Paul didn't get up or offer to shake hands; they never did.

"Hot," Dundee said by way of greeting. He was plump and shiny, the hair carefully combed across the baldness of his pink scalp. Spherical enough to appear boneless. In the beginning Paul had taken him for a heavy-handed and painfully sincere paperwork man, but the air of unsophistication was a ruse and there was a sly sense of humor inside. It was evident now. Dundee had a look of satisfaction, almost glee. "I've gone to war."

"Against the revenuers?"

"The computers. I picked this up – thought you might want to read it. Maybe I can recruit you."

Dundee put the book down on the desk and Paul turned it around to read the title. *Guerrilla Handbook for Computer Haters.*

"Read it," Dundee said. "I've already started my campaign. I paid the Con Ed bill this morning. Made out the cheque for two cents less than the bill, and I cut two extra holes in the computer card. And I told Marjorie from now on all postage stamps go on sideways – it screws up their magnetized scanners." Dundee settled into the leather armchair at the corner of the desk. He glanced out toward the East River and seemed ready to make a remark about the visible smog but didn't; Dundee was a New Yorker and unlike Sam Kreutzer he didn't need to talk about the city. He said, "You busy right now?"

"No, I just walked in."

"Oh, that's right, you had lunch with their majesties the Arizona clients today. How'd it go?"

"I think we'll get to handle the audit."

"I knew you were the best one to go. You to do the soft sell and Sam to dazzle them with figures and jokes."

"I'm not even sure I want the job. Mergers like that can be messy. Remember the Bradshaw thing?"

"It gave Mel Gregson his first coronary. I could hardly forget it. Incidentally I ran into Bradshaw Junior the other day at the Harvard Club." Dundee shook his head sadly. "The blood does thin out from generation to generation. He's got no macho at all. Remember the old man?"

"Bradshaw? No, he was before my time."

"Hell you're not that young. You're as old as I am. He only died twelve years ago."

"I meant it was before my time with the firm. I was still downtown then."

Dundee did an oh-yes-I-forgot, stupid-of-me frown. "Somehow you give the impression you've been here forever, Paul. I don't know if that's a compliment or not.

12

Anyway about young Bradshaw — funny, he's at least forty-five but he's still Bradshaw Junior to everybody around here. He buttonholed me with a big brag about how he made ten thousand dollars last month by selling short when the slump started. He made some wise remark like 'Only a fool holds out for top dollar.' No class at all, this second generation. The old man, now, he was something else. You must have heard the stories."

"A few."

"One of the real men. He got his start down in Houston by reclaiming old bricks from buildings that were undergoing demolition."

"I never knew that."

"Most people don't. Everybody seems to think he just went out at the age of seventeen and scratched a hole in the dirt with a stick and struck oil. Not Bradshaw. He made his capital the hard way and then he *bought* his way into the oil business. But by God the man knew what money was really for."

"Did he?"

"The first year he hired us to do his returns he listed seven girls on a single expense voucher and claimed he'd spent a total of four thousand dollars on them — and he told me privately he was being conservative on the voucher." Dundee shook his head in remembered admiration. "I remember one time he paid a Nieman-Marcus model three thousand dollars to take a shower naked in an oil gusher at one of his wells. I think I've still got the photo clipping from the *Daily News*."

"Last of the big spenders."

"You don't know the half of it. Of course he kept a high-powered gang of press agents on big retainers just to keep his name out of the papers, in his last years, but he never slowed down. He used to paint New York like

13

nobody else – spend four, five nights in a row hitting shows and nightclubs like a cyclone. Never went to bed. Seemed to get along with a few cat naps on restaurant tables. He'd have two or three call girls in his suite around the clock so he wouldn't have to pick up a phone if he felt horny. And mind you this is when he was well into his sixties."

Dundee smiled faintly. "Course he was a brutal old son of a bitch, he had moss growing down his north side, but he had a lot of charm too. He was a member of the Metropolitan, the Union League, he had respectable people on his boards of directors. But by Christ the man had style. There's nobody around like that any more."

"Maybe it's just as well," Paul said drily.

"No. Nowadays we're all nothing but a series of seven digits. Unless we take up arms the computers'll grind the life out of any potential Bradshaws we may have left." A pudgy finger tapped the book on Paul's desk. "You read it. I bet you'll join up."

It seemed to conclude Dundee's anecdote-for-the-day; he cleared his throat and when he resumed it was in his getting-down-to-business voice. "Now. About Ira Nemserman. The damn fool's done it again."

"Oh Christ."

Dundee slid a couple of sheets of folded paper from his pocket and tossed them on top of the anti-computer manual. "Read it and bleed."

Paul had a look. Ira Nemserman was one of the self-made men. He had learned to count money in the millions but to him any numbers which weren't preceded by dollar signs were numbers that had to be computed on fingers and toes, and usually inaccurately. Obviously Nemserman had typed the two sheets himself – a capsule summary of income and outgo for the past quarter –

and someone, probably Dundee, had circled two items in red: a common-stock block purchase on January sixteenth and the sale of the same block on June nineteenth.

Paul said, "I don't believe it. I just don't believe it."

"He's a child. You know that."

"A filthy-rich child. It's not as if this is the first time."

"I think you'd better get him on the phone, Paul."

"God I'd like to wring his neck."

"Before you do, remember the size of the fees he pays us." Dundee got up to go. "And don't forget to read that book."

When Dundee was gone Paul reached for the phone and pushed the inercom button. "Get Ira Nemserman for me, will you Thelma?"

It was ten minutes before she buzzed him back. "I have Mr. Nemserman for you now?"

"Good girl."

"Benjamin?"

"Mr. Nemserman," he said wearily. "Where are you?"

The voice sounded like lumps of concrete rattling down a construction chute. "Steam room at the gym. What can I do for you?"

"Can you talk?"

"Sure I can talk. I get no secrets from anybody. You ought to know that – you're my accountant, haw."

Paul closed his eyes and squeezed his temples. "Mr. Nemserman, I've got your quarterly figures in front of me here."

"Good. I did a nice job for you this time. Everything organized good and neat. Hell, Benjamin, I do three quarters of your work for you – you ought to cut your fee, you know that?"

15

"That's funny, Mr. Nemserman, because I was just thinking about doubling it."

"Haw."

"You've got a problem."

"Will you listen to this. *He* tells *me* I've got a problem. Benjamin, right now I've got so many problems that if anything else happens today it'll be at least ten days before I can worry about it. What with the Dow Jones down more than eight points today, the Exchange Index down thirty-six cents –"

"Mr. Nemserman, you're trying to claim a capital gain on this block of Conniston Industries, is that right?"

"So?"

"You bought it January sixteenth, you held it until June nineteenth, and you sold it for a gain of four hundred and forty-two thousand dollars."

"That's what it says on my paper, don't it?"

"Yes, sir. That's what it says. You're sure there's no mistake about those dates? You couldn't have written June when you meant July?"

"Now why the hell would I have waited for July when the stock was up that high in June?"

"Mr. Nemserman, from January sixteenth to June nineteenth is precisely five months and three days."

"*Five* mon – oh my God."

Paul rolled his eyes toward the ceiling. "That's right. You've declared a capital gain, and your tax on that would be a little over a hundred and ten thousand, but actually this is straight unearned income because you didn't hold the securities a minimum of six months. So your total tax bill on the sale is likely to run you somewhere around two hundred and seventy thousand more than you figured."

"Jesus H. Christ." There was a moment of silence,

16

either for thought or for prayer; finally Nemserman said, "What do I do about it?"

"Pay it."

"Nuts. I'd sooner go to jail."

"They probably could arrange that."

"Come on, Benjamin, you're the whiz kid. Tell me what to do."

"Well you probably know the dodges as well as I do."

"The hell. Who's got time to read all that crappy fine-print?" The man had an annual gross income in the neighbourhood of a million dollars and didn't have time to read the Internal Revenue Code. Paul shook his head. Nemserman growled, "What do you suggest?"

"Well of course you've got the standard gambits. Inflate your expenses grotesquely – they may buy part of it. You could cut thirty-five thousand off your tax bill by getting married, of course."

"Forget that."

"You could establish some trusts, taxable at the twenty-six percent rate. That would cut you back to the capital-gain level. It's a little late in the year to try that, but if you moved fast you might swing it."

"Yeah?"

"Or foundations. You can set up your own foundation and donate money to it, and then borrow the money back from the foundation."

"How do I do that?"

"IRS Form Ten-twenty-three. You fill it out and send it in to apply for tax-exempt charitable status. If you can make your foundation look religious or educational or charitable, you're in."

"What are you waiting for then? Set me up a foundation."

17

"It would be better if you had your lawyer do that, Mr. Nemserman."

"Oh. Yeah. Well, okay, Benjamin. Thanks. I'll get right on it. Christ they're bandits, these federal guys, you know that? Christ what a puking mess we're in in this country."

"Well maybe you'll get a sympathetic computer."

"Haw." Nemserman hung up on him without amenities and Paul leaned back in the chair filled with amused disbelief. After a moment he uttered a jocular bark of laughter. He laced his hands behind his neck and reared his head back lazily.

The smog was burning off the river and he saw a freighter fighting its way up against the current, screws churning the water. The electric plant was making a lot of smoke on the Queens side of the river.

The headache was gone; he felt good. Forty-seven years old, a little overweight maybe but in good health; all you really needed was a few laughs and with friends like Sam Kreutzer and Bill Dundee, and clients like Nemserman, the requirement wasn't hard to meet.

He reached for the stack in his In box.

The intercom.

"It's your son-in-law, Mr. Benjamin? Mr. Tobey?" Urgency in Thelma's voice. "He says it's an emergency?"

He punched the lighted button on the phone, more puzzled than alarmed. "Hello, Jack?"

"Pop, I – something's happened." Jack Tobey's voice was metallic – emotion held severely in check.

"What is it?"

"I don't – oh, hell, there's no way. Look, they got mugged. Right in the fucking apartment. I'm on my way over to –"

"Jack what the hell are you talking about?"

18

"They – I'm sorry, Pop. I'll try to make sense. I just got a phone call. Carol – and Mom. Somebody broke in, beat them up God knows why. They're taking them in an ambulance over to emergency receiving at Roosevelt Hospital – you know where it is?"

"On West Fifty-ninth?"

"Yes. I think – I think Mom's pretty bad. Carol told the cops to call me."

Cops. Paul blinked and gripped the receiver hard. "But what happened? How are they? Did you call Doctor Rosen?"

"I tried. He's out of town."

"My God. But what *hap*pened?"

"I don't know. I'm on my way up there. The cop was pretty brusque on the phone."

"But what –"

"Look, Pop, we'd better not waste time on the telephone. I'll meet you up there."

"All right."

He put down the phone and stared at the freckled back of his hand.

3

He followed the signs to Emergency and found Jack sitting tense with one shoulder raised, twisting his knuckles. Jack looked up without recognition.

"I'm sorry. My cab got hung up in traffic. You must have been here quite a while already." He felt he had to apologize to someone.

Jack said, "You may as well sit down. They won't let us in there."

People on the hard wall-benches sat holding minor wounds and invisible illnesses. The room had a smell and a sound; the sound was a muted chorus of agony but it was the smell that Paul couldn't stand. Hospital staff in dirty white clothes kept hurrying in and out. An empty ambulance pulled away from the open ramp. There must have been twenty people in the room, most of them sitting, a few rushing in and out, and except for one woman who sat blindly holding a little boy's hand, none of them seemed to pay any attention to one another. Pain was private, not for sharing.

A cop sat on the bench beside Jack. Paul sat down on the other side of him. Jack said, "The officer's kind enough to stay and see if he can help. This is my father-in-law."

The cop extended a hand. He had a tough black face. "Joe Charles."

"Paul Benjamin. Can you tell me – what's happened?"

"I was telling Mr. Tobey here. We didn't want to question Mrs. Tobey too much, she's pretty shaken up."

"What about my wife?" He said it quietly; he wanted to scream it. But you talked in muffled tones in a room full of strangers in anguish.

A man sat holding an injured arm against his belly, bleeding onto his lap. Paul wrenched his eyes off him.

The cop was saying, "We don't know. She was still alive when they took her out of the ambulance."

She was still alive – the implications of the cop's choice of words set the pulsebeat drumming in Paul's temples.

A young man in white came into the room in company with a nurse. The young man beckoned to the woman with the small boy. The woman took the boy by the hand and followed the intern and the nurse out of the room. The man with the injured arm watched them until they were gone. Blood kept soaking into his trousers. After a moment the cop said, "Excuse me," and got up to walk over to the man, dragging a handkerchief out of his pocket.

Paul stared at his son-in-law. Jack's face was grey. He didn't seem compelled to talk so Paul prompted him. "What did he say?"

"Not much." Too stunned to be drawn out? Paul tried again:

"Did you talk to Carol?"

"Yes. She didn't say much that made sense. She seems to be in shock."

"And – Esther?"

Jack shook his head. "Look, it's very bad."

"For God's sake tell me."

"They beat them both up."

"Who? Why?" He leaned forward and gripped Jack's wrist. "You're a lawyer. Think like one. Testify like a witness, can't you? Tell me."

21

Jack shook his head as if to clear it. "Pop, I just don't know. Two men, maybe more. Somehow they got into your apartment. I don't know if they broke in or if Mom or Carol let them in. I don't know what they wanted there. I don't know what they did or why, except that they – attacked – them both. Oh, not rape, I don't mean rape. That wasn't it. They just – beat them up."

"With their hands?"

"I guess so. There was no blood that I could see. I don't think they could have used knives or anything, there would have been blood wouldn't there?"

"Who called the police? You?"

"No. Carol called the police. Then the police called me."

"When did it happen?"

"I don't know." Jack looked at his watch and shot his cuff absently. "Couple of hours ago now, I guess."

Paul tightened his grip on Jack's wrist. "What about Esther? What did he mean, still alive?"

Jack's chin dropped; he stared at his shoes. "Pop, they – they must have twisted her neck as if she were a rag doll."

A nurse came in and touched the cop on the arm. "What are you doing?"

"Trying to stop the man bleeding."

"It's not arterial, officer. And it's better to let him bleed a little than to put an unsterilized handkerchief on the wound."

"Miss, I've seen enough cases of shock from loss of blood. Now I know you people are swamped. I'm only trying to help out."

"Thank you, then. That'll be all." The nurse took the injured man by the arm and led him away. The man looked over his shoulder at the cop but never changed expression.

The cop came back to the bench. Jack said, "What happened to him?"

"He was in a bar. Somebody broke a bottle in half and carved his arm. No particular reason – he didn't even know the man. These hot summer days people go a little crazy. But I guess you know enough about that." The cop seemed to feel an obligation to apologize for everything that had happened in the world. Paul understood how he felt. It was as if whatever happened was your fault and you ought to try and make amends.

Paul said, "Can you tell me anything about this?"

The cop said, "I don't know too much about it myself. Later on you could call the precinct. You want the number?"

"Please." Paul took out his pen and found a scrap of paper in his pocket – the American Express receipt from lunch. He wrote on the back of it as the cop dictated:

"Twentieth Precinct. Seven-nine-nine, four one hundred. The station house is right around the corner from your building, I don't know if you've noticed it. One-fifty West Sixty-eighth, that short little block between Broadway and Amsterdam."

"Who should I ask for?"

"I don't know who'll be in charge of your case. Probably one of the Detective Lieutenants."

"Who's the head man there?"

The cop smiled very slightly. "Captain DeShields. But he'd only refer you down to whoever's in charge of the case."

"Do you mind telling me whatever you do know?"

23

"It's not much. I wasn't the first one to get there. It looks like some men got into the building without the doorman seeing them. Maybe they were junkies, they usually are. Looking for something to steal."

"How did they get into our apartment?"

"Afraid I don't know. If the door wasn't double-locked they could've slipped the lock with a plastic card. Or maybe they just knocked and your wife let them in. Burglars often do that – knock to find out if anybody's home. If nobody answers the door they break in. Otherwise most of them make up some lame excuse about being on the wrong floor, and go away."

"But these didn't go away."

"No sir, I guess not." The cop's delivery was impersonal, as if he were testifying in court, but you could feel his compassion.

Paul said, "They got away," not a question.

"Yes sir. We still had patrolmen searching the building when I left, but I don't think they'll find anyone. It's possible somebody saw them in the building or on your floor. Maybe somebody rode with them in the elevator. There'll be detectives over there, they'll be asking everybody in the building if they saw anyone. It's possible they might get descriptions. Anyhow I imagine your daughter will be able to describe them as soon as she's feeling a little better."

Paul shook his head. "They're never found, these animals. Are they?"

"Sometimes we catch them."

Paul's glance flicked belligerently toward the doorway to the corridor. For God's sake when were they going to tell him something? He was beginning to fill up with undirected anger but he wasn't ready to think about revenge yet.

24

The cop said lamely, "They're doing everything they can." It wasn't clear whether he meant the detectives or the doctors.

There was a loud groan. It could have been any one of a dozen people in the room. Paul wanted to bolt to his feet and force his way through the door; but he wouldn't know where to turn once he got past it. And someone would throw him out.

The rancid stink was maddening. After a while – he wasn't reckoning time – the cop got to his feet clumsily, rattling the heavy accoutrements that hung like sinkers from his uniform belt. The thick handle of the revolver moved to Paul's eye level.

The cop said, "Look, I shouldn't have stayed this long. I've got to get back to my partner. But if there's anything I can do, just call the station house and ask for me, Joe Charles is my name again. I wish I could've been more help."

Paul looked up past the revolver at the cop's hard young face. Jack reached up to shake the cop's hand: "You've been damned kind."

They sat endlessly waiting for Authority to come and speak. Jack offered him a cigarette, forgetfully; Paul, who had never smoked, shook his head. Jack lit up the new cigarette from the glowing stub of the old one. Paul glanced up at the No Smoking sign but didn't say anything.

On the opposite bench a woman sat in evident pain but she kept stolidly knitting at something yellow; a man's sock? A child's sweater? Her face was taut and pale. Whatever her malaise she managed to clothe it in dignified resistance to fate. Paul felt like a voyeur; he looked away.

25

Jack muttered, "They may have been kids you know. Just kids."

"What makes you say that?"

"We get them every day at Legal Aid. They're out of their heads, that's all. They'll swallow ten of everything in the medicine cabinet and shoot up whatever they can lay their hands on."

"You think these were hopped up?"

"Well that's an obsolescent phrase, Pop, it doesn't exactly apply any more. Maybe they were tripping on speed or maybe they were junkies overdue for a fix. Either drugs they'd taken or drugs they couldn't get – it works both ways."

"What's the point of speculating?" Paul said bleakly.

"Well, it's the only thing I can think of that might explain this. I mean there's no rational motive for a thing like this."

"We always have to make sense out of things, don't we."

"Something happens like this, you have to know why it happened, don't you?"

"What I'd like to know," Paul answered viciously, "is why it couldn't have been prevented from happening."

"How?"

"Christ I don't know. There ought to be some way to get these animals off the streets before they can have a chance to do things like this. With all the technology we've developed you'd think there'd be some way to test them psychologically. Weed out the dangerous ones and treat them."

"A couple of hundred thousand addicts in the streets, Pop – who can afford to treat every one of them as long as we go on spending seventy percent of the budget beefing up weapons to overkill the rest of the world?"

26

You sat in a dismal emergency waiting room and talked tired generalities. It always came around to that. But neither of them had any real heart for it and they lapsed quickly into fearful silence.

It was the kind of place in which you did not look at things; you avoided looking. Paul's eyes flicked from the door to his knotted hands and back again.

Jack got up and began striding back and forth, too vinegary to sit still. One or two people glanced at him. Interns and nurses came in, got people, took them away. An ambulance arrived with a stretcher case whom two attendants carried straight through into the corridor. Esther and Carol must have been brought in like that, he thought. Possibly the theory was that if you were able to navigate into the place on your own feet you were healthy enough to wait six hours. Paul felt his lip curl; he straightened his face when a nurse appeared but she had come for someone else.

Jack sat down with a grunt and lit a new cigarette. The floor around his feet was littered with crushed butts. "God. I can't take this. Poor Carol – Jesus." A quick sidelong glance at Paul: "And Mom. What a rotten –"

Paul put his elbows on his knees and held his head between his hands, feeling as if it weighed half a ton.

Jack said, "At least they could talk to us. Damn it, how much would it cost them to send someone out here for a minute and a half to tell us what's going on?"

Paul stirred. "You're sure they know we're out here?"

"I talked to the doctor when we got here. He knows."

"Well I suppose he's got a lot of emergencies back there."

"He could send *some*body."

It was childish and Jack seemed to realize that; he

27

subsided. Paul slumped back against the wall and watched smoke curl up from the cigarette. "What's this doctor like?"

"Young. I suppose he's a resident."

"I wish we could have got Doctor Rosen."

"They're always out of town when you need them. The son of a bitch is probably playing golf in Putnam County."

"In this heat?"

Jack waved his cigarette furiously; it was his only reply.

Paul had taken a long time to warm to his son-in-law; he still felt uncomfortable with him. Jack came from New Mexico, he regarded the city as a reformer's personal challenge, he approached everything with humorless earnestness. *What a strange way to think at a time like this.* If ever there was a time to take things seriously. . . . Perhaps it was because he needed an object for his rage and Jack was at hand.

Carol had sprung Jack on them: an elopement, the marriage a *fait accompli*. Esther had always set a lot of store by ceremony; her unhappiness had fueled Paul's dislike for the young man. There had been no need for them to elope, no one had prohibited the marriage; but they had their own ideas – they claimed they'd run away to save Paul and Esther the expense of a big wedding; actually it was more likely that they simply thought it a romantic thing to do. They had been married by a Justice of the Peace without friends or family present. What was romantic about that?

Carol had gone on working as a secretary for the first three years to support them in a Dyckman Street walkup while Jack finished law school at Columbia. It had made things hard for Paul and Esther because there was no

28

way to be sure how much help to give them. They had the pride of youthful independence and accepted things with graceless reluctance as if they were doing you a favour by accepting help from you. Perhaps they felt they were. But Paul had spent twenty-three years being unapologetically protective toward his only child and it wasn't easy to understand her cheerful acceptance of that Dyckman Street squalor. The kind of place you couldn't keep cockroaches out of. Fortunately when Jack had passed the Bar exams and got the job with Legal Aid they had moved down to the West Village to be nearer his office; the apartment was one of the old railroad flats but at least it was more cheerful.

Jack had the zeal of his generation. His dedications were more compassionate than pecuniary; he was never going to be wealthy but he would support Carol well enough; probably in time they'd buy a small house on Long Island and raise babies. In the end Paul had accepted it all, accepted Jack – because there was nothing else to do, because Carol seemed content, and because he began to realize it was lucky she hadn't taken up with a long-haired radical or a freaked-out group of commune crazies. She had the temperament for it: she was bright, quick, pert, impatient, and she subscribed to a good deal of anti-Establishment sentiment. Probably she had tried various drugs in college during her two years of student activism; she had never volunteered a confession and Paul had never asked. She had a good mind but her weakness was a tendency to be sold by the last person who talked to her: sometimes she was too eager to be agreeable. Jack Tobey probably exercised exactly the kind of steadying influence she required. It would be silly to hold out for more than that.

Jack wore glasses with heavy black frames across his
29

beaky nose; he was dark and shaggy and he dressed with vast indifference – most of the time you found him in the jacket he was wearing now, a hairy tweed the colour of cigarette ashes. Scuffed brown shoes and a bland tie at half-mast with his shirt open at the collar. Paul had seen him in action in the courtroom and it had been one of the few times he recalled seeing the kid in a business suit; afterward Carol had explained that Jack made the concession to decorum only because he had got to know the judges and their habit of exercising their prejudicial sarcasms on unkempt young defense attorneys.

... A plump young man in white appeared at the door and it made Jack stiffen with evident recognition. The doctor located him and came forward. "Your wife will be all right." He was talking to Jack.

Paul stood up slowly and Jack said, "How's my mother-in-law, Doctor?" in a voice that presupposed the answer.

Paul cleared his throat. "May I see her?"

The doctor's head skewed around. "You're Mr. Benjamin? Sorry, I didn't know." It was an apology without contrition. The doctor seemed jaded; his voice was rusty, tired beyond any expression of emotion. He seemed to need to ration his feelings.

"I don't –" The doctor's round young face tipped down. "Mrs. Benjamin is dead. I'm sorry."

4

At the funeral he was still in a dark fugue, a dulled pervading unreality.

It was the wrong day for a funeral. The heat had dissipated, the inversion layer had gone somewhere; it was a mild day filled with sunshine and comfort. Funerals had a rainy association for Paul and the chiseled clarity of Friday's air made the incidents even less real.

That first night – Esther had died Tuesday – they had sedated him and he only vaguely remembered the taxi ride to Jack's apartment. Jack had given him the bed and in the morning Paul had found him in the living room on the couch, smoking, drinking coffee; Jack hadn't slept at all.

Paul had emerged from his drugged sleep neither rested nor alert. The unfamiliar surroundings heightened his sense of existential surrealism: it was as if he had been born fully grown half an hour before, into an alien world of meaningless artifice. He had forgotten nothing; but when he found Jack in the living room and they began to talk, it was as if they were actors who had sat in these same places and said the same lines so many times that the words had lost all intrinsic meaning.

The city coroners had sent someone around to obtain Jack's signature on an autopsy-permission form which Jack disagreeably pointed out was a senseless absurdity since in crimes of violence that resulted in death it was automatic to perform a post-mortem examination. The Medical Examiner had announced that the body would be released on Thursday; to which funeral home should it be sent?

Trivial mechanical details. Decisions to make. Should there be a religious service? If not, how did you go about conducting a burial ceremony?

She had not been religious; neither was Paul. They both came from religiously indifferent backgrounds, nominally Jewish, effectually disinterested. Even their political causes and charitable interests had been non-sectarian; they had never supported Zionism or the Temple or the B'nai Brith.

But in the end Jack had telephoned someone and got the name of a rabbi.

They did it because it was the easiest solution and because Esther had always been comforted by ceremony. "It's the least we can do," Jack had said somewhat obscurely – what more could be done for her now? – and Paul had acquiesced because he had no reason to object, and no energy for dispute.

You preserved a modicum of sanity only because there were so many idiotic decisions you had to make. When was the funeral to take place? The burial? Whom should you ask to attend? In the end he found that the funeral director took care of most of the details and the rest sorted itself out: their closer friends telephoned and after accepting their condolences with as much grace as he could produce, Paul told them the services would be held Friday at two-thirty, gave them the address of the funeral home and listened numbly to their repeated expressions of sympathy.

Still he was surprised by the number of people who put in appearances. The rabbi, who had never met Esther, spoke briefly from a simple dais in a chapel-room in the mortuary. His remarks were dutiful and innocu-

32

ous; afterward they all went out onto the kerb on Amsterdam Avenue and there was a fairly well directed confusion of finding seats in limousines and organizing the vehicles of the cortege in the proper order. Sam Kreutzer and Bill Dundee stopped on the way to their cars to touch Paul on the arm and speak murmured words. Several people from the office were there and he was surprised to see a client there – George Eng, the Chinese Executive vice-president of Amercon, with whom he and Kreutzer had lunched Tuesday.

Two couples from their apartment house came; and there were various cousins and nephews and nieces from Manhattan and Queens; and Esther's sister-in-law from Syracuse, representing Esther's brother Myron who had a minor diplomatic post in Malaysia and had been unable to come. He had, however, sent the largest of the floral arrangements.

Paul found himself standing at the graveside cataloguing the attendance as if there were some point giving good marks to those among their acquaintances who had chosen to appear here.

The casket had been closed from the outset; there had been no viewing. Paul had not seen her since he had left the apartment Tuesday morning; she had been following the vacuum cleaner from room to room. He felt no desire to view her remains and had suffered impatiently through the "mortuary scientist's" obsequious explanations of why it would be best to do it this way. Boiled down it amounted to the fact that she had been mauled badly by the attackers and the autopsy surgeons had cut her up considerably, and while it was possible for the morticians to put her back together, it would be expensive and unsightly. On the way out of that meeting Paul had been surprised when Jack had made a bitter remark

33

about "plastic surgery on the dead"; it was not Jack's usual tone, it betrayed his strain. Throughout the week Paul had been quite alert to other people's behaviour, he had observed their reactions to the events without ever wholly observing his own. It was as if reaction was still to come: he existed in a hiatus of emotion, waiting for the explosion or the crash or the tears, whichever it was to be. He half expected to go off like a Roman candle.

Jack stood beside Carol, holding her arm. Carol was stiff in protest against all of it. Like her father she had not yet come out of it; unlike him she had withdrawn into an obvious shell. Her eyes windowed resentment more than anything else. She looked terrible, he thought: she stood with a caved-in posture, her hair hung damp and heavy against her face. Ordinarily she drew the second glance of most men but now she looked old, hard, furious: as if she were nobody's daughter.

Possibly it was partly the result of the drugs. She had been under sedation for most of the first three days because whenever they stopped dosing her she would tighten up like a watchspring and if you touched her, her rigid body would jerk galvanically. Yesterday he had reached for her hand, trying to make contact; her hand was ice-cold and she had pulled it away, clamped her lips shut, averted her face. She hadn't gone into total shock – she could converse quite rationally, in a voice that lacked its usual expressiveness – but Paul was worried about her. Jack had agreed she might need psychiatric looking-at if she didn't pop out of it in another day or two. Perhaps after the funeral she would begin to loosen up.

The casket was in the grave, the ropes had been with-

34

drawn; the rabbi stopped talking and people began to drift away. A few came by to speak to Paul or to Carol; most of them – the ones who were discomfited by other people's suffering – left quickly, trying to look as if they were not hurrying away.

Henry Ives, the senior partner in the firm, stopped to say, "Of course you needn't come back to work until you feel up to it. Is there anything we can do, Paul?"

He shook his head and said his thank-yous and watched Ives hobble away toward his waiting Cadillac, a bald old man with age-spots in his skin. It had been kind of him to come; probably he disliked these reminders more than most did – he was at least seventy-three.

Jack said, "We may as well go."

He stared down at the casket. "I guess so."

"Are you sure you wouldn't rather stay over here for a few days?"

"No. You don't really have room. It'd be crowded – we'd be on each other's nerves," Paul said.

He sensed Jack's relief. "Well, just the same. At least stay the evening. We'll whip up something out of the freezer."

In this poor indoor light somehow the bruises under Carol's makeup were more evident. She sat down on the couch, crossed her legs and leaned forward as though she had a severe pain in her stomach. "I'll fix something in a little while."

"It's all right, darling, I'll do it."

"No." She was snappish. "I'll do it myself."

"All right, fine. Just take it easy." Jack sat down by her and put his arm around her shoulders. She didn't stir.

35

"Maybe we ought to call Doctor Rosen," Paul suggested.

It brought her eyes around against him. "I'm perfectly all right." She shot to her feet and walked out of the room, moving heavily on her heels. Paul heard things crashing around in the kitchen.

"All right," Jack muttered. "Let her get it out of her system." He looked around. "I'm half surprised the place hasn't been ransacked."

"What? Why?"

"Burglars always read the obituaries. They know nobody's going to be home at the time of the funeral."

"In broad daylight?"

"Most break-ins happen in daylight. That's when people aren't home. These guys that attacked Mom and Carol – that was in broad daylight."

Paul shed his black suit jacket and sat down in his shirtsleeves. "Does she have a better recollection of it yet? Does she remember what they looked like?"

"I don't know. She still doesn't want to talk about it and I haven't wanted to press her. She remembers it, of course – she's not amnesiac. But she's repressing it with everything she's got. It's only natural."

"Yes. But the police need something to go on."

"I talked to Lieutenant Briggs this morning on the phone. We're going to take her up there Monday morning to look at their mug books and see if she can pick them out."

"Has she said anything at all about it?"

"The other night she talked about it a little. When the Lieutenant came to the hospital. I was pleased how gentle he was in his questioning. He managed to get things out of her that I couldn't. A real professional – I wish there were more like that guy."

36

"What did she say?"

"Evidently there were three of them. Young men, probably teenagers. She said they – laughed a lot. As if they were hysterical."

"Drugs?"

"I suppose so. It must have been. Either that or they were totally psychotic, but anybody who behaves like that all the time wouldn't still be on the streets – they'd have been picked up a long time ago."

"Did she tell you how they got into the apartment?"

"She told Lieutenant Briggs. I gather Mom and Carol had just come back from the supermarket. They got back up to the apartment and a few minutes later somebody knocked at the door and said he was the delivery boy from the market. When she opened the door this kid was standing there with a big cardboard carton. Mom thought it was the groceries so she let the kid in. The minute he was inside the door he dropped the carton – it turned out to be empty, the cops went over it for fingerprints but paper doesn't take prints very well, all they found were smudges. Anyhow the kid pulled a knife and his two friends shoved into the doorway behind him. One of them grabbed Carol and the other two started punching Mom, demanding to know where she kept her money."

"We never keep much money in the apartment."

"She only had three or four dollars in her handbag – she was planning to go to the bank later that afternoon. And Carol only had ten or eleven dollars and a few subway tokens. We've been kind of watching our budget lately, we just bought this furniture and the payments are a bit more of a load than we thought they'd be."

"So," Paul said slowly, "when it turned out there wasn't more than a few dollars in the place they flew into a rage, is that it?"

37

"That seems to be what happened. They must have been strung out on amphetamines, that's the way it sounds. Evidently they giggled and laughed the whole time. Carol said that it was the worst thing about it – they never stopped laughing. I think the reason they didn't – hurt her as badly as they hurt Mom was that when she saw what they were doing to Mom it got to be too much for her and she passed out. Naturally she doesn't remember anything that happened after that for a while. When she came to her senses they were gone. She had the presence of mind to get to the phone and call the police."

Paul was grinding a fist into his palm. "They took the portable television and a couple of other things. You'd think someone would have seen them carting those things out of the building."

"Evidently not. The three kids must have been hanging around the supermarket and saw Mom and Carol come out without any packages. That would indicate they were having the groceries delivered. Then the three kids probably followed along to the apartment house. You know the way that doorman of yours always greets you by name? So it wouldn't have been any trick for them to find out Mom's name – the doorman chirping at her, 'Hello, Mrs. Benjamin,' and the building directory right there by the front door with everybody's name opposite a doorbell button. So they found out her name and apartment number, and then Lieutenant Brigg's best guess is they went around on Seventy-first Street down to that condemned tenement building half way down to the dead-end. It'd be no big deal to get into that building and through the basement into that big courtyard behind your building. Then all they'd have to do would be to break into the basement of your building. It's not the first time burglars seem to have used that route to get into the building. If

38

I were you I'd talk to the super about putting locks and bars on those basement windows."

"That'd be locking the barn after the horse has been stolen."

"It's not the last time somebody's ever going to try breaking into that building, Pop. It's happening every few minutes in this pressure cooker we all live in."

Paul nodded vaguely. "It's just so hard to believe. That's what I can't get into my head – such a senseless God damned murder."

"Well I doubt it was premeditated, Pop. I don't think anyone kills with his hands unless he's angry or drugged to the point of irresponsibility. Not this way."

Paul felt it come: the quick steady blast of blinding rage. He said through his teeth, "Is that how you'd defend them?"

"What?"

"Your grounds for their defense. They weren't responsible for their actions." He put on a savage mimicking tone: " 'Your Honour, they didn't know what they were –"

"Now wait a minute, Pop."

"– doing.' Now God damn it I don't give a shit what you call it, this is deliberate cold-blooded murder and if you think –"

"I don't think," Jack said coolly, "I know. Of course it was murder."

"Don't humor me. I've seen you in court trying to make innocent victims out of your slimy guilty little clients. I don't –"

"Pop now you listen to me. Whoever did this to Mom and Carol, they're guilty of first degree murder. It's the law – the felony murder law. Any death that results from

39

the commission of a felony is first degree murder even if the death was an accident, which God knows Mom's death isn't. They were committing a felony – assault with intent to commit robbery – and they're guilty of Murder One, guilty as hell. My God, do you think I'm arguing against that? Do you honestly think I'd –"

"Yes I think you would!" He hissed it with furious force. "Do you think your fine neat pigeonholes of legal technicality can explain away all this? Do you really think these savages deserve all that complicated fine print?"

"Well then what would you suggest?" Jack was cool, soft, deliberate. "Catch them and string them up from the nearest rafter, is that the idea?"

"It's better than they deserve. They ought to be hunted down like mad dogs and shot on sight. They ought to –"

"Pop you're just working yourself up. It's not doing anybody any good. I feel the same way you do. I understand exactly what you're going through. But they haven't even caught these bastards yet and you're already jumping to the conclusion that some smart lawyer's going to get them off the hook. What's the use of aggravating things with useless speculations? They haven't got these kids, for all we know they never will get them. Why get so upset about miscarriages of justice that haven't even happened yet?"

"Because I've seen the way these things work. Even if the police catch them they just go right out again through the revolving door – right back out onto the streets. And largely because of well-meaning bastards like *you*! Hasn't any of this even made you stop and think about what you're doing?"

"It's made me stop and think," Jack said. He turned

40

his glance toward the kitchen. "Let's just let it go at that for the moment, shall we?"

"What are you kids made out of? If I were you I'd have handed in my resignation two days ago and put in an application for a job on the District Attorney's staff. How can you conceive of going back to your office and going right on defending these filthy little monsters?"

"It's not all that simple and you know it."

"Do I?" he demanded. "Isn't that maybe our biggest failing? Copping-out with the complaint that it's not all that simple? By God maybe it *is* all that simple and we just don't have the guts to face it!"

"So you'd like to just strap on a pair of cowboy six-guns and go out there and gun them down, is that it?"

"Right now," Paul said, "that is exactly what I'd like to do. And I'm not a hundred percent sure it's the wrong idea."

"My ears are pretty good, you don't have to shout."

"Sorry," Paul snapped.

Jack sat there in his rumpled black suit, his hair standing out in wild disorder; his eyes mirrored a bitterness that Paul understood and felt.

Paul kept his eyes on Jack's face too long; it made Jack get up and move to the liquor cabinet. "You want a drink?"

"I could use one."

"Bet you thought I'd never ask." Jack's smile was too brief. He opened the cabinet door and poured two glasses half-full of Scotch. No ice, no mix. He handed one to Paul and went back to the couch. "I'm sorry if I seemed patronizing. I guess I was trying to be reassuring – not because it would calm you, but because with all this desperation in the air I needed calm words myself. Does that make sense?"

41

"Of course. I'm sorry I blew up." But they were talking like cautious strangers now. He didn't know which was worse.

Jack said, "All week I've been remembering something that happened – oh, two-three years ago. It must have been after midnight. I'd been up in midtown on some chore, something to do with a client, and it was a nice night so I was walking home. I ran into a teen-age girl outside Bryant Park. She was a wreck. It turned out she'd been gang-raped right there in the park. I gave her carfare and told her to call the police. I don't suppose she ever did."

"Why not?"

"She was kind of flippy. Probably being gang-raped wasn't exactly her idea of a fate worse than death. She was sore at them, but not really mad. You know what I mean?"

"I can't say I do, altogether."

"What I guess I'm getting at is that so many of these things simply aren't taken seriously any more. Or at least they're taken for granted. Do you know what that girl said to me? She said she should have known better than to go into Bryant Park at that hour. She almost seemed to think it was her own fault. She wouldn't have been raped if she hadn't gone there. It's a weird time we live in."

"Are you trying to say," Paul breathed, "that Carol's mother invited this to happen by something she herself did?"

"Not at all. Don't fly off the handle again. I suppose if both of you had lived as if you were in a besieged fortress – use the peephole religiously, never let a stranger inside the apartment, put extra locks on the doors, never travel outside the apartment without a vicious guard

42

dog on a leash – I guess if you chose to live like that she might still be alive, but who can put up with that?"

Paul knew people who did.

"Look Pop, I know this won't set well right now, but in time you're going to have to think of it as a tragic accident – as if a disease had struck her down, or a runaway bus on the street. It's no good getting worked up into demands for vengeance and retribution. Even if they catch these three bastards and put them away for the rest of their lives it won't really change anything."

Paul waited for the inevitable *It won't bring her back* but Jack never uttered it; perhaps after all he was not totally insensitive to the more blatant clichés.

"We both have to face that," Jack droned on relentlessly. "In these times you have to feel inadequate if you can't slip a door-lock open in three seconds with a plastic calendar card – every kid on the street can do that. Do you know the crime statistics? I hear them every other day from some sourpussed Assistant D.A. There's an assault or a robbery every twelve seconds in New York – something like seventy thousand reported cases last year, and that's probably less than half the number that didn't get reported. In felony cases they only make arrests in about one-sixth of the cases and of those they only get convictions on about one-third. Of course in murder cases it's a lot higher – the police usually solve about eighty percent of them, but still we have about three murders a day in the city. You and I and Carol and even Mom – we're statistics now. On that God damned blotter. That's what makes it so damned hard to maintain your personal perspective. To you and me this is the most devastating thing that's ever happened – to the cops it's something they see all the time, so often they just can't keep getting worked up about it."

43

Paul felt acid. "Thank you, Jack, you're a balm and a consolation to me."

"I'm sorry. I didn't mean to sound like a wise ass. But I'm in this business, I guess you could say – at least I'm on the periphery of it, I have to deal with the police every day. And I think you've got to be prepared for the possibility that nothing more is ever going to develop in this case. You've got to go on living haven't you?"

"No," Paul said slowly, "you don't have to go on living."

"I don't want to hear any more of that."

He stood splayed with the drink in his hand. His lowered head swung back and forth like the head of a worn-out prelim fighter in the ring, trying to locate his opponent. "I'm not thinking about suicide, I didn't mean that." But he kept bulling it, thinking. His breathing was shallow; his sphincter contracted, he formed a loose fist. "I've never hit a man in anger in my life. Never called a black man 'nigger' or stolen a penny from any man. I've given money and my own time to a dozen worthwhile causes from block associations to the N-Double-A-C-P."

"And this is the thanks you get," Jack murmured. "I know Pop. And it's true, and there's no answer to it."

"There's one answer I intend to demand. I want those three killers."

"They'll probably get them. They may not. But if they don't, what do you plan to do? Turn your back on every decent principle you've ever stood for? Join the Birchers or the Ku Klux Klan?"

"Well, I don't know what I'd do," Paul said vaguely. "But Christ there ought to be *some*thing."

"You mean like hire a private eye? Or get a gun and

44

go looking for them yourself? Those things only happen on television, Pop."

"Well, just the same you may have hit on something there. A private detective might be –"

"Private detectives aren't what the movies make them out to be, Pop. They exist for the purposes of getting divorce evidence and providing security services like industrial counter-espionage and bank guards. There are no private eyes who investigate murder cases, and even if there were they wouldn't be able to hold a candle to the police. At least the police have manpower and organization and know-how."

"And total indifference."

"I wouldn't say that. You remember that policeman who stayed with us at the hospital?"

Paul even remembered his name: Joe Charles. "He was only a uniformed patrolman."

"Sure. But he's a human being. He does care, Pop. Some of them are corrupt and some of them don't give a shit, but the cops aren't really the pigs we made them out to be in college."

"Like unto thee and me," Paul growled. "It doesn't change the fact – if your estimate is correct – that there's an excellent chance these animals will never be brought to justice."

"Justice – or revenge?"

"What difference does it make what you call it?"

Jack shook his head. "All I'm saying is you and I may never be able to do a thing about this. Obviously we can't go out into the streets and find these killers ourselves. We wouldn't begin to know where to look."

"Then you're saying we should just forget the whole thing. Go back to bed and pull the covers up over our heads."

"Or write letters to the *Times*."

It made Paul look at him; it was the kind of sarcasm you didn't expect of Jack.

"I guess you're right," Paul said. "I guess you're right."

"We may have to get used to it, Pop."

"I guess we can try."

5

He didn't sleep at all that night; but he hadn't expected to. There were chloral hydrate capsules if he wanted them. He didn't. He felt the longer he went on drugging himself out of it the longer it would take to purge himself of his demons. It was better to face them and have it out.

It was the first night he had spent in his own apartment since the murder. He had left Carol's apartment early, before the sun went down. He hadn't planned that, it had come out of an argument: Carol somnambulistically had served up something barely edible and the three of them had sat down to it listlessly. They pushed food around on their plates and said very little. Once Jack got up to put a Mahler recording on the stereo; a few minutes later he got up again and took it off. No music would have been right for that hour – heavy music intensified the despondency; trivial music would have mocked it.

In the circumstances none of them had the stomach for silence and so they had begun to talk: awkward, forced. The significant things were not to be said; it was bad enough having to think them. So they had attempted to make impersonal conversation but it was too much of a strain and inevitably the talk had come around to things closer to home: whether Paul would keep the apartment now, whether they should call the police to find out if anything had developed or whether they should wait for the police to call them.

In the end it had led to another argument about retribution *vs.* reality and Paul had got to his feet to make some angry point, his voice trembling, and Carol suddeny had covered her ears with her palms and screwed her eyes shut and uttered an earsplitting shriek.

"You'd better go on home," Jack had said.

"I'd rather wait till the doctor gets here."

"No, I think it would only upset her more. You can understand that."

Jack had given her a pill and put her to bed while Paul was calling Dr. Rosen; now Jack picked up Paul's jacket and handed it to him. "I don't mean to seem cruel."

"Damn it I'm her father."

"Right now you're a reminder of her mother, I think."

A sharp remark rose to his tongue – something acid about Jack's licence to practice parlour psychiatry – but he had let it die there; Jack was too vulnerable, there was too much heat already.

So he had left, bile in his throat. A taxi from Horatio Street to the upper West Side. He'd got out of a taxi at the corner of Seventieth and West End, crossed the avenue with the light and walked up the half-block to the apartment house, staring with belligerent suspicion at every face on the street.

The night man on the door gave him a nod and a polite smile of recognition as if nothing had ever happened. Was it possible he didn't know? Paul stopped automatically to unlock the mailbox. It was crowded with small stiff envelopes – sympathy cards. He shoved them in his pocket, locked the mailbox and went along the corridor from the lobby to the back elevator. He rode up partway with a middle-aged couple he'd seen often enough to say hello to; he didn't know their names. If they had seen the papers they hadn't made the connection; they nodded and said goodnight when they got out at the seventh floor, leading their Pekingese on a leash snuffling and tugging. Paul rode on up to the twelfth floor, put the key in the lock and pushed into the apartment with his stomach muscles tensed, not sure what he was going to find or how he was going to react to it.

Someone had slid a note under the door. It lay askew on the carpet. He bent down to pick it up, ready for anger, half expecting it to be a threatening letter from the killers. It was a sympathy card from the Bernsteins next door. He put it together with the stack from his pocket and left the pile on the end-table under the mirror in the foyer.

They had moved into this apartment after Carol had started college and it had become regretfully evident that she was no longer going to live at home with them for any extended periods of time. There was only the living-room, middle-sized, and the large corner bedroom and bath, and the kitchen off the entrance foyer. The building was forty or fifty years old, it had the high ceilings and multitudinous closets of its vintage, the curious moldings that ran around the walls a foot below the ceiling, the Edwardian ceiling-light fixtures. It wasn't quite old enough to have a bathtub on claw feet, but the bathroom had that flavor to it. It was a small apartment but comfortable, it had more than its share of windows and most of them looked down upon the attractive row of converted brownstones on the opposite side of Seventy-first Street.

He kicked the door shut behind him and glanced into the kitchen and walked into the living-room. The place had been tidied; everything was neat. Had the police gone to the trouble? It wasn't the cleaning lady, she

49

came on Mondays. He scowled; he had expected to find wreckage, he had occupied himself thinking about cleaning the place up.

The flavour of Esther was in the place but it didn't seem to affect him. He walked through the rooms trying to feel something. It was as if his subconscious was afraid to let him feel anything.

Something unfamiliar caught his eye and it took him a moment to figure out what it was. He had to run his eyes around the living room and study each object. The chairs, the coffee table, the bookcase, the television, the air-conditioner in the window. . . .

He went back. The television. The killers had stolen the television.

It was a console; it stood in the corner where the old portable had squatted on its table. It looked like a color set – the kind with built-in stereo and AM-FM radio. He crossed the room in four long strides.

There was a note:

> *Paul–*
>   *In hopes this may make it just a*
> *bit more bearable –*
>   *Our very deepest condolences,*
>   *–The Guys at the Office*
> *P.S. – We stocked the refrig.*

It broke him down: he wept.

They had never had a color set and he hadn't seen many color programmes – only the occasional badly tuned football game above a bar, and once or twice the Academy Awards on some friends' enormous set. He spent twenty minutes fiddling with the thing, tuning in all channels, trying to find amusement. He was too restless. He switched it off and thought about making a drink, but decided against it.

The phone rang. It was Jack. "Dr. Rosen just left. He's prescribed some stronger sedatives. He's arranging an appointment for her with a shrink Monday morning."

"Well, I suppose that's the best thing right now."

"I hope it'll help snap her out of it. I imagine it will. Rosen says he's got a very good man."

"I imagine he would."

"It was damned nice of him to come. Where can you find a doctor willing to make house calls on Friday night any more?"

"He's been our family doctor for almost twenty years."

"Well I'll let you know if anything changes. Right now she's asleep – doped up. The poor kid. Christ this is a rotten thing. . . . How about you? Are you all right up there? You can still come back down and spend the night if you'd feel better. I know it must be miserable up there all alone."

"I'll have to get used to it sometime. This is as good a time to start as any."

"There's no need to make it too hard on yourself, Pop."

"I'll be all right," he growled. "I'll probably drop by tomorrow to look in on Carol."

"Fine."

After he hung up the apartment seemed emptier. He reversed his earlier decision and made a drink. Carried it into the bedroom and sat down, jerked at his tie, bent down and began to unlace his shoes.

He kicked them off and reached for his drink and heard himself cry out.

He couldn't believe it. He had always managed to

51

bottle things up; anything else was weakness. He sat like a stone, writhing inside, experiencing terror from the crazy random impulse to do violence: he wanted to smash out at anything within reach.

Finally he began swinging his fist rhythmically against the side of the mattress. He got down on one knee and swung from the floor. It didn't hurt his fist and it didn't do the mattress any damage and after a little while he knew there wasn't going to be any satisfaction in it. He remembered a kid in high school who'd put his fist through the panel of a door in one of the study halls – all the way through it. He couldn't remember whether the kid had done it on a dare or just out of sheer rage; the kid had been one of the athletes, a bully everyone feared. Paul thought about slugging a door but he was afraid of pain, he didn't want to break his hand.

A hammer, he thought. That would feel good – taking a hammer to something, swinging it as hard as you could.

And do what? Smash up the furniture? The walls?

His brain kept frustrating him.

In the middle of the night he got up and took a shower. Lying on the bed drying off, he wished Esther were there. He would have shouted at her and it would have made him feel better.

Just last week he had noticed how overweight she was getting – the way the flesh of her sapless breasts and her armpits was bunched around the edges of her bra; how thick her hips had become, her waist and thighs, the soft heavy padding of flesh under her chin. Well she was forty-six years old, a year younger than Paul, almost to the day they were both Aquarians.

Aquarian acquaintances, he thought. All the intense

52

promises when you were youthful; but after marriage they had settled into their lives without any sparks. They had slowly got fat and out of shape. They had both been strangely old before they should have been – as if they had never been young.

In the beginning she had been an attractive girl who moved gracefully and had a soft voice, mercifully lacking in the brass that coated the tongues of most of the city girls he met. He supposed they had liked each other from the outset. They had gone on liking each other. There had been surprisingly few fights; he knew they both had been repressed people who had to build up a head of steam before being able to give vent to their rages, and by the time things became that intense there was usually some outside outlet – the office, the community volunteer groups where Esther worked almost full-time and Paul had contributed as much time as he could spare.

Now with hindsight he was unhappy with the feeling that they had both played life too carefully. Was he sad now because he had loved her, or because he was guilty that he hadn't loved her? Nothing left now but a fistful of lost dreams – but then they were dreams that had been lost long ago; her death perhaps was nothing more than a punctuation mark. It had been, most of the time, a good quiet friendship – not what they had dreamed of in the early days, but perhaps the highest possibility either of them was capable of attaining. They did not blame each other for things; yet when he saw friends and acquaintances who adored their husbands or wives, he remembered his envy.

Now what would he do with himself on the week-ends?

It hadn't been a Technicolor marriage but she had become a condition of his life. It was important to have someone. He began to understand what his father, who had lived alone a good part of his life, had endured.

It came again: a shortness of breath, a debilitating rage that flooded all the tissues of his body.

He disentangled himself clumsily from the twisted sheets and went into the bathroom, switched on the light and stared at himself in the mirror. His ginger hair was getting very thin on top. The freckles that covered his cheeks and hands seemed to have multiplied and intensified to the texture of knockwurst. His eyes were in red pouches; he saw the flabby lines in his face and throat, the beginnings of a sagging pot in his belly that pulled creases into his sides along the ribs. A washed-up, used-up carcass. He walked into the kitchen, moving nothing but his legs; poured a new martini ten-to-one, not bothering with ice, and padded back into the living-room. When he sat down he realized it was the first time he had moved naked through the apartment in years. They had both failed to overturn their pristine and modest backgrounds; they always changed clothes in the bedroom, they never walked naked through the living-room and kitchen.

Chills swept him furiously. He took the top magazine off the unread pile beside the couch; opened it at random and read a long paragraph and went back to start it again, realizing he had not paid attention to the meaning of the words. After the second try he gave it up and closed the magazine.

This wouldn't do. He had to *do* something: he had to start making some sort of plans.

He decided he would call the police in the morning. Maybe they had to be needled.

He swallowed half the martini and looked around the room with a different glance: trying to picture how it

54

had happened. Where had they done it? On the carpet? Right here on this couch? He tried to visualize it.

It was hard to form a picture. He had never seen real violence except on television or in the movies. Until this had happened, he had been secretly convinced that a good part of it was fictitious – part of the spurious hearty masculine myths that city men constructed to reassure themselves of their *machismo* and the toughness of the world they inhabited. Intellectually he knew better but in his private emotions and fantasies he did not really believe, in a personal way, that hoodlums and killers existed. He had lived his entire life in the Sin Capital of the world, except for the two years they had lived within commuting distance of it, yet never with his own eyes had he seen any vice or corruption, or any violence beyond the occasional arbitrary explosion of a motorist or pedestrian so overcome by inarticulate rage that he began to shout at taxi drivers and beat their fenders with fists. He had never seen a bookie, never known a gangster. He knew drugs were pushed in the neighbourhood: one block east was Needle Park, and he had seen the faces full of listless ennui which he understood belonged to addicts, but he had never seen drugs change hands, never seen a hypodermic needle outside a doctor's office. Sometimes he had been frightened by the harsh laughing packs of teenagers who roamed through subway trains and stood in knots on street corners, but he had never actually seen them commit acts of violence. Sometimes it was hard to escape the feeling that the pages of the *Daily News* and the *Mirror* were filled not with fact-news but with the lurid fantasies of pulp-fiction writers.

He knew plenty of people whose apartments had been burglarized. Once, three or four years ago, Carol's purse had been snatched by a quick nimble arm darting through a closing subway door. Those things happened but they happened anonymously; there was no real feeling of personal human violence to them.

Now he had to get used to an entire new universe of reality.

6

There was a crime story in the Sunday *Times Magazine* and Esther's name was in it. Sam Kreutzer called at ten that morning to tell him about it. "How are you getting along?"

"I'm all right."

"It's a rotten time. Is there anything at all we can do, Paul?"

"No. Nothing."

"Maybe you'd like to come over and have dinner with us one night this week."

"Can I let you know later on in the week, Sam? Right now I don't much want to see anybody." He wanted to evade the kindnesses of friends. It hadn't happened to *them*; it was secondhand to them. You only bled from your own wounds. There was a saccharine quality to people's sympathy, they couldn't help it, and pity was a cruel emotion at best.

He called Jack. Carol was still asleep. Paul said he'd telephone again later; he probably wouldn't come there to eat unless she was feeling much better – otherwise a rain-check?

He went out to buy the *Times*. Walked up the avenue to Seventy-second and over to the newsstand by the subway station on Broadway. It was quite warm. He narrowly watched the flow of people on the streets, wondering for the first time in his life which of them were killers, which were addicts, which were the innocent. Never before had he felt acutely physically afraid of walking on the streets; he had always been prudent, used taxis late at night, never walked dark streets or ventured alone into uninhabited neighbourhoods; but that had been a kind of automatic habit. Now he found himself searching every face for signs of violence.

He carried the *Times* back along Seventy-second Street, walking slowly, consciously looking at things he had spent years taking for granted: the filth, the gray hurrying faces, the brittle skinny girls who stood under the awning in midblock. There wasn't much traffic – on these last warm Sundays after Labor Day everyone fled the city, seeking to prolong the summer as much as they could by soaking up sunshine in the country or at the crowded beaches.

A woman stood staring vacantly into a display window of one of the cheap variety shops. There was a red sign in the window: *¿Cómo sabe Vd. que no tiene enfermedad venérea?* How do you know you haven't got V.D.? She was a primitive woman, her dark face mottled with scars, her mouth loose: an ancient slut, an evil hag with a greasy shopping bag pendant from her doughy hand. How many killers had sprung from her loins? How many muggers had lain between her ancient yielding thighs?

He rushed back to the apartment, alarmed.

Monday he was still deep in what he decided was post-trauma *tristesse.* He had taken sleeping pills last night; they made him irritable in the morning. Last night he had decided it would be best to go in to the office today – even if he didn't get any work done it would be better to have familiar people around him – but now he knew he couldn't face any of them.

He went to the bank because he was low on cash. It was a short walk, across the street from the newsstand on the corner of Broadway and Seventy-second. The same route he had followed yesterday to buy the *Times*; the same route he had followed thousands of times, to and from the subway to go to work. Yet now it was different. He slipped into the bank as if it were a hiding place.

He had thought of buying a heavy cane and carrying it as a weapon. But it would be unwieldy at best; someone with a knife could get in under it, and it might anger them if they saw you carrying an obvious club.

At the counter he stood behind a fat man in a grease-spotted apron who was buying change, probably for a lunch counter's cash register. The man went away with a sack heavy with coins wrapped in paper rolls.

Paul bought a ten-dollar roll of quarters. Back in the apartment he slipped it into a sock, knotted it, and crashed it experimentally into his cupped palm. Then he put it in his pocket. He would carry it all the time henceforth.

He wasn't gentle; he was a flabby coward. It was dawning on him that the most terrifying thing about his existence was his ineffectualness.

He felt like a fool. He took the roll of coins out of his pocket, untied the sock, and went to put the roll of quarters away in the drawer of an end table. The drawer opened an inch and then stuck. He jerked at it; it came out, fell from his hand, tumbled on to the rug. The oddments from it – safety pins, decks of cards – flew across the floor.

He blurted a string of oaths at the top of his lungs.

After he had put the drawer back and gathered up its droppings he re-wrapped the roll of quarters in the sock and returned it to his pocket.

59

He called a locksmith and the man agreed to come round Wednesday and change the locks, replace them with heavy models that couldn't be slipped with cellulose or broken by pressure.

For several hours he sat constructing fantasies of methods of boobytrapping the apartment against intruders. Shotguns with wires attached to the triggers. Grenades.

After that he began to call himself names: stupid idiot, paranoid fool.

Jack phoned a little after five. "I've been trying to get you since noon."

"I had the phone off the hook. Too many sympathy calls."

"I know what you mean."

"Did Carol see the psychiatrist?"

"Yes, we went around there this morning. He seemed like a nice guy, pretty level-headed. He prescribed some tranquillizers and said she'd probably take a little while to get over it. I think he spent more time talking to me than he spent with Carol. A lot of speechifying on how I have to be calm and patient and understanding with her until she's over it. You'd think she was pregnant."

"It sounds as if he's probably right, though. Aren't you relieved?"

"I was at the time. But she's incredibly depressed, Pop. She hardly reacts at all when I talk to her. It's like talking to a wall."

"Maybe that's partly the effect of the tranquillizers."

"Maybe," Jack said without conviction.

"Do you think it would do her any good if I came around to see her?"

"No. I mentioned it to the doctor. He said it might be better for her not to see you for a little while. I told him you might be hard to convince, but he seems to feel it's important to try and protect her from certain associations with the crime. Evidently she identifies you with it because it was your apartment. Now please don't misunderstand, Pop – it's not that she blames you for anything. But it might be better if you didn't see her for a few days."

"That's what he said, is it?"

"Yes. I'm sorry – I know things are hard enough for you without –"

"Never mind, I understand." He wasn't sure he did, altogether; but he didn't want to start an argument. It would be fruitless. "Well I'll call you tomorrow." He rang off, feeling dismal.

He had called the police Sunday morning; he phoned again Monday evening and was put through to a Lieutenant Malcolm Briggs. "Yes, that's right, Mr. Benjamin, I'm in charge of the case."

"I was just wondering if anything had developed. Any – leads."

"Well I'd like to be encouraging but right now we haven't got anything strong enough to call a lead. We've pinned down one or two people who saw a group of kids hanging around the front of the supermarket at about the right time of day that afternoon. One of our witnesses says he thinks he'd recognize them if he saw them again, so if we do pick them up he'll be able to do a show-up for us. But so far no one's been able to pick them out of our mug books. Your daughter looked through the mug pictures yesterday of course, but she wasn't positive enough about any of the faces to identify them."

"I didn't know she'd been to police headquarters."

"She wasn't. I talked to Mr. Tobey, he told me her condition, so I managed to talk the deputy inspector down there into letting us have a couple of patrolmen relay the mug books over to her at her apartment, one at a time. She went through all our photo files of people who've had records of anything close to this kind of modus operandi. As I say, she didn't pick any of them out. She did give us something of a description, though."

"Oh?"

"She seemed to be pretty sure that two of them were Puerto Ricans and the third was black. Of course he may have been a black Puerto Rican – there are quite a few of them."

"Well isn't there a method you people use of reconstructing faces with drawings of various features?"

"The Identikit, yes, sir. She didn't seem to feel up to that."

"Well, she should be feeling better within a few days."

"She can have a crack at it whenever she's ready, sir."

After the connection broke, Paul thought of half a dozen more questions he should have asked. He brooded at the telephone, then dialed the Horatio Street number.

"Jack?"

"Oh hello, Pop. Anything wrong?"

"Why didn't you tell me Carol had been through the police mug books?"

"I guess it must have slipped my mind. I mean she didn't recognize any of them."

"It must have been damned upsetting for her."

"She insisted on it, Pop. It was her idea."

"Judging by what's happened I don't think it was such a good idea."

"Well at the time I thought it was an encouraging sign

62

that she had the gumption to want to do it. Afterward it only seemed to make it worse, though." Jack's voice cracked slightly: "Hell Pop, what are we going to do?"

He wished he had an answer.

When he hung up he realized why Jack hadn't told him about it. Jack had anticipated an explosion; he knew how protective Paul could be.

It made him wonder why he hadn't exploded more forcefully than he had. Things were still bottled up inside him, under high pressure. Something was bound to burst.

7

On Thursday Carol was hospitalized at Columbia-Presbyterian for observation; at least that was what the psychiatrist called it.

By Thursday morning Paul had begun to realize how dangerous it was to coop himself up alone. The longer he spent in the apartment the more terrifying the outside world became. He had to bestir himself. It was too easy to seal himself off, stare at imbecilic television programs and blank walls. Drinking more than he ate. Getting no exercise at all. He kept thinking he was having heart attacks.

Except for the hours when he tried to sleep he avoided the bedroom. It was too full of Esther. He knew he should pack her things and get rid of them but he didn't want to go near them yet so he confined himself to the living-room, the kitchen, the foyer; sometimes striding back and forth from one to the other but usually sitting blankly in front of the television console whether it was turned on or not.

He had only been out of the apartment three times on brief excursions in the past one hundred hours. That was no good. The body rotted, the mind deteriorated; only the demons of subconscious fantasies thrived.

He decided to call Sam Kreutzer at the office and take Sam up on the invitation to dinner if it was still open; he prepared himself for the possibility that Sam and his wife would have some other engagement for tonight, and reached for the phone.

It rang before he touched it. Jack, to tell him about Carol's hospitalization.

Paul didn't remember the conversation clearly afterward. He knew he had shouted at Jack – damn fool questions to which Jack couldn't possibly have the answers; cruel inane accusations that only succeeded in eliciting chilly replies from Jack. Finally Jack hung up on him.

He hadn't even got the psychiatrist's name. He would have to call back and get it. But not right away; he had to give Jack time to cool off first – and give himself time for the same thing.

He showered – scrubbed himself viciously until the flesh stung with a red rash. Shaved with meticulous care. Got into a completely clean set of clothes from the skin out for the first time in five days. His best office suit – the grey gaberdine Esther had insisted he buy in the Oxford Street shop the last time they had been to London, three years ago. He knotted his tie precisely and fixed it to his shirt with the silver tiepin. Wiped off his shoes with a rag. Checked himself in the mirror, re-combed his hair, and braced himself to walk out the door.

In front of the building spinters of shattered glass lay like frost on the sidewalk – a broken bottle. He stepped around it and looked both ways for traffic and jaywalked across to the east side of the avenue. When he walked up Seventieth toward Broadway the children were leaving P.S. 199, making a racket, traveling in packs and knots. His stomach muscles knotted. At first he didn't look any of them in the face – as if by pretending they didn't exist he could prevent them from seeing him. He let them flow around him. There was a lot of rough-edged laughter in high voices. Did it have a savage brutal ring to it or was he only hearing it that way?

As he forged into the midst of the yelling mass he suddenly began looking them straight in the faces. In his pocket his fist closed around the knotted sock, weighted with its roll of coins.

One tall youth caught Paul's glance. The youth's eyes flickered when they touched Paul's: flickered and slid away. Paul almost stopped. His head swiveled to follow the youth, who said something to the kid beside him; they both laughed but they didn't look back in Paul's direction.

He had the light at the corner; he trotted across Amsterdam and was stopped by the light at Broadway so he turned right on the kerb and began to walk toward Columbus Circle. He was out of the packs of kids now; his gut relaxed. But his thoughts raced: what had he expected? To be attacked in the midst of a street crowded with schoolchildren? To get into a stare-down match with that tall youth, and come to blows?

You have got to get hold of yourself.

He approached the clean attractive buildings of the Lincoln Center complex. A sudden impulse sent him across Broadway on Sixty-fifth and he went into Central Park, heading across town.

Just inside the park a bum staggered near with palm outstretched; and Paul, who had always felt obliged to pay off the infirm ones, hurried past with his face averted.

The park was covered with the leavings of callous humanity: discarded newspapers, crumpled lunch bags, rusty bottlecaps, rustless empty cans, broken bottles. Several years ago he had worked an entire summer, every spare hour of it, for the volunteer anti-litter campaign. *All right, they've been told, they've had their chance.*

He didn't follow the implications of the thought through: he was afraid to.

Near the zoo a drunk sat swaying on a bench. His eyes tracked Paul. He looked as if he had no past and was entitled to no future. He kept watching Paul, his head turning to follow Paul's passage. It set Paul's teeth on edge. He hurried through the zoo and out onto Fifth Avenue.

He had started with no particular destination, only an urge to get out, get moving, put an end to his unhealthy isolation. By now he knew where he was heading. He quickened his pace even though his feet were beginning to get hot and sore.

The door sucked shut behind him. Marilyn the receptionist, who was a matronly twenty-six-year-old brunette with the suggestion of a double chin, did a double-take that contrived to combine in one expression amazement, pleasure and sympathy. "Why Mr. Benjamin!" she chirped. "How nice!" Then she remembered; her face changed with comic abruptness. "Oh we were all so *fright*fully sorry to hear . . . Poor Mrs. Benjamin . . . It must have been just *ter*rible for you –"

He nodded and muttered something and hurried through the corridor door before she could take a notion to suffocate him protectively against her big soft bosom.

He went along to Sam Kreutzer's office and got a similar reception from Sam's secretary; when he went into the office Dundee was with Sam. They were both effusive; it was a while before he could get a word in. "I was getting cabin fever. Thought I'd come back to work. I'm probably not much good for anything yet but it might help just to sit there and push papers around."

"I think you're dead right," Dundee said. "At least you'll have some friendly faces for company."

He steadied himself against the banal predictability of their throat-clearing and face-rearranging. Sam said, "Hell, Paul."

Dundee gripped his arm with one hand and patted his shoulder with the other. "It always takes a while, fella, but we're all a hundred percent with you. Anything you need, anything at all. . . ."

"It's okay, Bill." He endeavored to lighten things: "Actually, Sam, if that invitation's still open, the one thing I think I really need more than anything else is a square meal. I've been living on frozen food – TV dinners that taste like reruns."

He wasn't sure if he imagined it: the briefest discomfiture on Sam's face? But a smile chased it away. "You bet, Paul. I'll call herself and tell her to set a place."

It bothered him: was Sam really chagrined? Did he feel it would be awkward? Maybe Paul shouldn't have asked. . . .

"I know exactly what you mean," Dundee was saying. "That time Anne was in the hospital, the kids all away at school – I was never so happy as when she got home and on her feet again. I suppose it makes me a male chauvinist pig, but I swear to God they bulk that frozen dreck with sawdust and castiron filings."

A smell was bothering Paul; sicksweet and thick. He finally ascertained it was Dundee's barber-shave.

Dundee's smile had gone rigid – as if he had just realised his anecdote had been misplaced. Anne had come home from the hospital after her operation. Esther

68

would never come home again. It was what Dundee was thinking: he always wore his thoughts on his face: and Paul couldn't think of a way to dispel Dundee's guilt without making things even more tedious and awkward than they were already. The best thing to do was overlook it, pretend he was oblivious to it, press on. He said as quickly as he could, "I began to get the very distinct feeling things around here were starting to fall apart in my absence. So I have returned. Partly to see whose fingers I might catch in the cookie jar –" a laugh, too loud and hearty, from Dundee "– and partly to start undoing all the damage you guys must have been doing to my clients' affairs."

Sam Kreutzer said, "As a matter of fact we were talking over one of your clients just now when you came in. Nemserman. Son of a bitch really got his tail caught in a crack, didn't he?"

"Has he been bugging you?"

"He calls every day or two, wanting to know how soon you'll be back in harness. He told me to convey his sympathies, by the way."

Paul wondered if that was true. He doubted it; Nemserman lacked that brand of consideration. Probably Sam had made it up on the spur of the moment because it was something that ought to be said.

Dundee said, "I talked to him yesterday – Sam was out when he called. He must've been calling from some bookie joint – the background noise was unbelievable."

"What'd he have to say?"

"Number one, when was Paul Benjamin going to quit sitting on his ass and get back to work. I'm quoting more or less verbatim. Number two, he seems to have learned a lesson – temporarily anyway – from getting stung on that unearned income he thought was a capital gain. He

69

instructed his broker to double-check back with him for six-month spans every time he takes a notion to sell a block of stock. Number three, he said this problem has brought to mind another difficulty and he wanted to discuss it."

"And did he?"

"Well, yes. I don't mean to get sly with your clients, Paul – I've put all of them off, I'm not trying to steal your people away from you. But Nemserman's been hot under the collar for the past week. I finally broke down and gave him the advice he was looking for."

"Advice about what?"

"Well, he's got a suitcase full of blue-chips he's had for a thousand years. I mean he's been holding some of the damn things since Roosevelt's first administration."

"Franklin," Sam Kreutzer said drily, "or Teddy?"

Dundee said, "If he sells the things now, of course, he'll have to pay a whopping capital gains tax on the increment. Some of those things have gone up in the past forty years, counting splits and stock dividends, from ten dollars to six hundred dollars. He was desperate to find a way to avoid paying out all that loot."

"What'd you tell him?"

"Told him to establish some trusts and sink the stocks into the trusts. Then just hang onto them. If he keeps them until he dies they'll pass on to his heirs, and the heirs can sell it without paying capital gains tax. And if he puts the stocks in trust for his heirs, it'll help get around some of the estate taxes."

Dundee was talking too much and too fast. Paul tried to set him at ease. "That's exactly what I'd have told him, Bill. Don't worry about it. I don't think he'll take your advice anyway, but at least he won't be able to complain later that we fouled him up."

70

Sam Kreutzer said, "Why won't he do it?"

"Far as I know he's only got two heirs – a sister and a nephew – and he hates their guts."

"Then why doesn't he set up a charitable foundation?"

"I've been trying to talk him into that for years. He keeps saying he'll get around to it. He never will. Hasn't got a charitable bone in his body."

"So he'll leave it all to two people he hates, and let the Government grab most of it on inheritance taxes. Well, I doubt he gives a damn what happens to it after he's dead. It's all monopoly money to guys like Nemserman. It's the way they keep score in the games they play. Once Nemserman dies and the game ends, who cares what happens to the chips?"

Dundee said, "I wish I could afford to look at it that way."

Paul settled into a chair. "Maybe he's right. There are times I'm convinced there's nothing more to existence in this world than a black desert where blind people pick up rocks and grope around to kill one another."

He hadn't meant to get onto that; it had been on the back of his tongue and he had let it slip out. When he saw how they reacted to it he regretted having spoken. Dundee was suddenly busy trying to find a neutral corner on which to settle his attention and Sam Kreutzer fixed his stare against the knot of Paul's necktie and said, "Well sure, Paul, I guess we know how you feel. I imagine things will look a little less bleak to you as time goes by."

"I doubt it," Paul said – evenly, without force; he didn't want to get into a heated dispute but he felt there were things inside him that needed airing. "Remember that piece in the Sunday *Times Magazine*? We read those things all the time but we don't really buy them. You don't believe these things actually happen – not until they happen to you personally."

"You can't blame people, Paul. They're exposed to it night and day – they get jaded with it. It's like crying 'wolf' – people hear about crime in the streets so often and so regularly that it ceases to have any meaning for them. And maybe that's a good thing. We all need some kind of defence mechanism – otherwise we'd all be stark raving mad."

Carol. . . .

Deliberately he forced himself forward. "Sam, it's got to have some kind of effect when you read how even seeing-eye dogs are having nervous breakdowns from the strain of living in this city. They're knifing policemen right in the precinct squad rooms – doesn't it *mean* something that in the city of New York you can't walk into some police stations without ringing the doorbell and waiting to be buzzed in?"

"Why do you think we're trying to find a place to live outside the city?" Sam's implication was clear.

"Maybe that's the answer, I don't know. Maybe – maybe Esther would still be. . . ."

"Oh Christ, Paul, try to take it easy, will you?"

"I'm all right. I'm not about to break down all over your carpets, Sam. It's just that I've been doing a lot of re-considering these last few days. It's not easy to realize that you just may have dedicated a good part of your life to a group of causes that turn out to be dead wrong."

Sam shook his head. "I can't believe that, Paul – and neither will you when you've had time to settle down and put this vicious thing behind you."

The conversation wasn't continued until that evening because Paul's reply was cut off by the arrival in Sam's

72

office of Henry Ives, the senior partner. "Marilyn told us you'd come in. Glad to see you, Paul – glad to see you."

Paul shook the knobby old hand. The rigidity of Ives's coin-slot mouth was a clue to his unease. "I can't tell you how sorry we all are over this terrible thing, Paul – sorry and angry. Angry right down to the soles of my feet, to tell you the truth. The fact that our so-called public servants allow these things to happen and keep allowing them to happen over and over again –" he drew a shuddering long breath to continue "– it's a source of bitter shame to all of us, Paul. Do they know anything about these hoodlums? I understand they haven't caught them yet. A disgrace, an utter disgrace."

The shift in topics almost caught Paul unawares; once Ives launched into a set-piece he almost invariably continued at length until it had run its course: Ives held himself with the religious fervour of the passionate egoist and all his posturings and attitudes were long and well rehearsed.

"No," Paul said, "they haven't turned them up yet. They're still working on it. I've been keeping in touch with the police. They do have one or two leads."

"Well by God they'd better act on them. I understand it was a group of young ones – teen-age thugs, is that right?"

"Apparently so."

"A disgrace," Ives said again, and held up a finger as if to forestall an interruption, which no one had offered. "These young scum grow up in a welfare state where they see that violence goes unpunished and the old virtues are for stupid pious fools. What can we expect of them that's any better than this random vicious despair? These radicals keep arsenals in their attics and advocate
73

the overthrow of an economic system which has graduated more people out of poverty than any other system in history. They arm themselves to attack honest hard-working citizens like you and me, and to shoot down beleaguered policemen, and what happens? The public is propagandized into outrage over the behaviour of the police in defending themselves and the public!"

Behind Ives's back Sam and Dundee were exchanging bemused glances of tolerant patience; their occasional nods and affirmative grunts were not quite patronizing enough to alert the old man.

Things went on in their peculiarly arcane fashion, as if nothing ever changed; and perhaps nothing *had* changed for Henry Ives and the others. For Paul everything was different; the shape and colour of the world was changed completely from what it had been.

That night across the dinner table he said to Sam, "We're all born into this society congenitally naive, you know. And those of us who don't outgrow it become the liberals."

"Oh now wait a minute Paul, you can't –"

"But I can. I most certainly can. Who has a better right than I do?"

It was a question to which neither Sam nor Adele chose to reply.

"It came to me a little while ago what we really are, we liberals. We demand reforms, we want to improve the situation of the underprivileged – why? To make them better off materially? Nuts. It's only to make ourselves feel less guilty. We rend our garments, we're eager to show how willing we are to accept any outrageous demand so long as it's black, or youthful, or put by someone who thinks he's got a grievance. We want to appease everybody – you know what a liberal is? A liberal is a guy who walks out of the room when the fight starts."

"I think," Adele Kreutzer said in a light let's-clear-the-air tone, "we are witnessing the right-wing radicalization of Paul Benjamin." She had a strong voice; it went with her long narrow jaw. She was thin and dark and wore a faint aura of self-mocking melancholy. "Of course it's true there's no way to go on living in New York. The kind of bastards who do these awful things can only survive in cities like this – put them out in a country village and the exposure would be instantly fatal. There'd be no place for them to hide."

"You may be right," Paul said. "But I'm not sure running away is the only answer."

"I can think of another one," Sam said, and when he had both their attention he continued complacently: "Drop a ten-megaton nuke with the Empire State Building at ground zero."

"He's got it," Adele said gaily, "by George he's got it!"

Their clowning was weak but it made its point. For the rest of the evening Paul eschewed the subject but he found it hard to keep his mind on anything else; there were chunks of time when he let their conversation pass him by.

He left early, planning to be home by ten-thirty so that he could call Jack. The Kreutzers seemed relieved to see him go; it would be a while, he thought, before they invited him again.

Well to hell with them. He disembarked from the elevator and crossed the lobby, noticing that their doorman was nowhere in sight. *Anybody could just walk in.* His jaw crept forward. He went out onto Forty-fifth and searched the street for a cab but there was nothing in sight; the Kreutzers lived far over on the East Side near the U.N. complex and it wasn't a busy night-traffic area.

The air was clouded with a fine drizzle. He turned up his jacket collar and put his hands in his pockets and walked up toward Second Avenue, avoiding puddles and refuse. He stayed to the curb edge of the sidewalk because the buildings – parking lots, loading bays – were filled with deep shadows where anyone could be lurking. Only half a block from the lights and traffic of the avenue; but places like this seethed with muggers, he knew. Sour spirals came up from his stomach. His shoulders lifted, his gut hardened. One pace at a time up the gray street, raindrops chilling the back of his neck. His heels echoed on the wet pavement.

It was like running a gauntlet. When he reached the corner he felt he had achieved something.

Reflected neon colors melted and ran along the wet avenue. He crossed it and stood waiting for the roof-light of a free cab to come in sight. Waited several minutes but by then he knew it was going to be one of those nights when there wasn't a taxi anywhere in the world. He turned a full circle on his heels, making a sweep – nothing. Trucks, the occasional green bus headed downtown, big sedans rushing past with pneumatic hissings, occupied taxis.

A half block north of him a figure staggered into sight under the lights of a storefront: a drunk trying to avoid stepping on the cracks in the sidewalk. Coming right toward Paul. In fear he turned quickly and began to walk west along Forty-fifth Street.

It was early but the neighbourhood had a four-o'-clock-in-the-morning feeling. He didn't see anyone at all until he got near the corner of Third Avenue. A young couple came in sight, walking uptown, a pudgy fluffy young man in a flared jacket and a girl in belled slacks with straight hair down to her waist: liberated singles, carefully not touching each other, talking animatedly about something fashionable and banal. Perhaps they were deciding whether to go to her apartment or his; perhaps they had already reached the stage of sharing an apartment, their surnames connected by hyphenation on the mailbox. They looked as if they didn't like each other very much.

Paul waved at an approaching taxi. Its cruise-light was illuminated but it swished past him without slowing. He fought the impulse to yell at it.

He waited through four red lights before a taxi stopped by him. "Seventieth and West End," he said through his teeth; sat back and banged the top of his head against the car's fiberboard ceiling. Was it just taxicabs or were the rear seats of all modern cars impossible to sit in without slouching and cringing? Paul hadn't owned a car since they had returned to the city from their brief fling at suburban life; other than taxis the only car he had been inside in the past year had been the mortuary limousine.

Through the plexiglass screen that sealed off the rear compartment he had a bad view of the driver; he had an impression of a huge Negro head, a hard roll of dark flesh at the back of the neck. Neither of them said a word.

A red light ahead was out of synch and the driver avoided it by swinging left on Forty-seventh and heading across town. All along the block west of Eighth Avenue there were girls leaning against the walls in dark doorways. On Ninth Avenue there was a troubleseeking cluster of teenage kids with their hands inevitably in their pockets, faces closed up into an unbreakable apathy. Addicts? Perhaps it was just that nothing short of the most violent brutality excited them any more. They looked as if they were waiting to kill someone.

Would he have had the same thought two weeks ago? Probably not, he thought; probably he would have sensed their boredom and resolved to dedicate more time to the neighborhood athletic league: "What these kids need is an interest. We need to set up some ball teams. Now let's get a committee together and raise a little money for equipment."

It was no longer the answer. Why should play-at-war games attract them when they had real wars to go to?

These were new thoughts for him and he wasn't comfortable with them but they kept crowding everything else out of his mind. By the time they passed Lincoln Towers he was deep into a fanciful daydream about a ball-team of vicious teenagers to whom Paul was supplying high-explosive shrapnel grenades, disguised as baseballs, designed to annihilate teenage gangs.

He paid through the little tilt-slot in the plexiglass and got out on the corner. He was about to cross the street when his eye fell on a convertible parked in front of the supermarket. Part of the roof had been slashed open; it hung in gaping shreds. Probably there had been some item of minuscule value visible on the back seat; someone had pulled a knife, ripped the car open, reached in and stolen the object. People ought to know better than to park canvas-topped cars on the streets. . . .

He stopped, drew himself up. *What the hell kind of thinking is that?*

Do we have to give up every God damned right we have? Do we have to let them scare us into giving up everything?

Fallen rain gleamed on the street like precious gems.

He looked over toward the river – along the block, under the concrete of the West Side Highway. The lights of a boat were sliding past. Out there on the filthy river in a boat you'd be safe.

Safe, he thought. *And that's all we have left to shoot for?*

The light changed and he had crossed the street and stepped up onto the sidewalk before he saw the man standing in the shadows right by the corner of the building. Standing against the wall, shoulder tilted, arms folded, smiling slightly. A black man in a tight jacket and a cowboy hat. As lean and efficiently designed as a bayonet.

Paul's toes curled inside his shoes. His hair rose; the adrenalin pumped through his body and made his hands shake. They stood face to face with a yard of drizzling rain between them. The black man never stirred. Paul turned very slowly and put his foot forward and walked up the street with the sound of his heart in his ears.

A panel truck was parked in front of his apartment house, facing the wrong direction for the traffic; there was a police parking ticket on its windshield but it hadn't been towed away: someone had slipped a few dollars to someone. Paul stopped beside the truck and used its big outside mirror to look back along the street. The black man stood where he had been, indistinct in the shadows. Streaming sweat, Paul went into the building.

The man's smile: did he know who Paul was? Was he one of the ones who had killed Esther?

He was letting his imagination run away with him. *Come on, get a grip on yourself.* Kids, Carol had said. Teenagers. This guy was full-grown – he wasn't one of them. Probably his amusement had been purely the result of Paul's all-too-obvious fear; probably he was an intellectual, a playwright or a musician who'd just decided to post himself on that corner and see how long it would take the cops to roust him along – some sort of experiment to prove something about white bigotry.

Paul thought about going back outside and telling the guy it wasn't a very wise experiment. *If I'd had a gun in my pocket and you'd looked at me like that you might have been in a lot of trouble, fella.* It was only a fantasy; there was no possibility of his going back outside. He nodded to the doorman and went back to the elevator.

A common enough fantasy though, I'll bet. If I'd been there when that guy slashed that roof – if I'd seen it happen, and I'd been armed at the time....

8

"You wanted to see me, Mr. Ives?"

"Have a seat, Paul."

Ives was the remaining survivor of the three nimble-penciled accountants who had founded the firm in Nineteen Twenty-six. It had moved uptown in stages from Beaver Street to Forty-third. The old man's office was a repository for oddments of decor from each of the firm's stopping places. An antique stock-ticker, a pair of grandmother clocks and four hideous gilt cherubs as wall decorations. The furnishings were pleasantly mismatched, the products of several different decades and levels of company prosperity: in one corner sat a modern Danish chair, a mock-Victorian step-end table, and a brass floorlamp from the 'Twenties with a plain cheap shade.

It was a huge office, plushly carpeted, occupying five hundred square feet of corner space with enormous windows on both exterior walls – a good view of the U.N. Building and the East River.

Paul pulled a chair forward and sat. Ives said, "How's your daughter getting along?"

"Not much change from last week, I'm afraid."

"A crying shame," the old man said. "I certainly hope she pulls out of it."

"The doctors have every confidence she will."

"Yes. Well. Still I expect you're very worried and anxious about her."

"Yes, naturally."

"There *is* something I can do to help – or to be exact, to help you to help yourself. That's why I asked you to come by. It's a job for you, and there ought to be a sizeable bonus in it if everything works out as it should. I'm sure the hospital expenses are quite heavy for you – I realise you've got that major-medical policy, but all the same there are always considerable expenses the insurance won't cover."

"Yes sir, that's quite true. I've had to dip into our little securities portfolio."

"Then this ought to help handily."

"I appreciate your consideration, Mr. Ives, but I'd prefer not to accept charity."

"Nothing of the kind, Paul. You'll earn it." Ives had his elbows on the leather arms of his high-backed swivel chair. He steepled his fingers and squinted, making it clear he was going to be strictly business about it. "Of course it's this Amercon situation. I had a call from George Eng this morning. Their board of directors wants to proceed in the direction he outlined to you a few weeks ago."

"A merger with Jainchill Industries, you mean."

"Yes. Howard Jainchill was here in the city last week and George Eng had several meetings with him. Everything seemed to go reasonably well, but of course they can't sit down to do any serious dickering until the two companies have examined each other's books. Naturally that's where we come in, as Amercon's accountants."

"We're to go over the Jainchill figures."

"Yes, quite. Of course the Jainchill home-office is out in Arizona."

Paul got a very straight look; Ives went on: "I

82

thought, frankly, a trip away from the city might be good for you at this juncture."

"Well, I hadn't thought about it but it might be a good idea," Paul said uncertainly.

Ives seemed to be waiting for a rider to the statement. When Paul added nothing the old man said, "Well then that's settled, you'll fly out with George Eng the end of next week."

"It's very kind of you, Mr. Ives, but on a matter this big shouldn't one of the senior members handle it?"

"Not necessarily. It's your kind of job."

"Well I'd like to be sure it's not going to – cause friction."

"Paul, I'm not concerned with doing a favor for you, except tangentially. You have a keen eye for other book-keepers' elastic accounting methods, you've always been willing to call a spade a spade. You handled the Masting case last year, so you're a bit more up-to-date on this particular variety of merger than most of the rest of the members. And you –"

"Excuse me, Mr. Ives, but in the Masting case we knew they were cooking the books and it couldn't help give us an edge – we knew what to look for. Are you suggesting the Jainchill people are doing the same thing?"

"I wouldn't put it past them." Ives said it with a tiny smile on his strict mouth. "I don't know Jainchill personally but he's got a reputation for being a man with the business ethics of a bankrupt car dealer."

"Do the people at Amercon suspect anything specific?"

"Not according to George Eng. But Jainchill knows Amercon's been sniffing around his company for quite some time. He'd be a fool if he hadn't done a bit of juggling to inflate his profit picture. Everyone does it when he's trying to promote a merger.

"Now we do know, for example, that for the past year Jainchill has been reducing the rate at which he's been writing off the cost of new plant facilities – he switched from rapid to straight-line depreciation. Naturally it reduced the amount he had to set aside on his books to reflect the deterioration of plant and equipment. You'll want to look into that to ascertain the real figures and find out how much it increased their reported profits.

"When it comes to deciphering the footnotes that clutter up corporate reports, there isn't a man in this office any better than you. It's a sure bet Jainchill's earnings reports look fatter than they really are. The question is, how much fatter? Basically that's up to you to ascertain, but you'll also want to look for all the other likely possibilities. Amercon has to have a clear picture of what they're buying before they'll make an offer for it."

"Of course."

"Then you're all set. I only wanted to make sure you were feeling up to it – it will be a tough job, Paul. It's going to take all your time for several weeks. I wanted to check with you this far in advance because you have to be certain you're willing to be away from your daughter for that period of time and ready to devote your complete attention to it."

He hadn't been allowed to see Carol anyway. The trip away from the city might clear his head; things were pressing in on him. "I'll be glad to do it, Mr. Ives. I'm grateful for the opportunity."

"We'll go over the details with George Eng before you leave. You've got a couple of weeks to prepare yourself. I know you'll do a fine job with it, Paul – I've always had every confidence in you."

Paul walked in relief to the door. When he glanced back across the length of the room Ives had a copy of the Revenue Code open and was scowling furiously at it.

9

"Well, you got pretty good hinges on this door," the locksmith said. "Lucky. Some of these newer buildings, they got hinges you could bust with a toothpick."

The first locksmith with whom Paul had made an appointment had failed to show up. It hadn't occurred to him at the time and he'd forgotten it for a while. He'd called this fellow two days ago – a squat bald man with a cauliflower ear and feral eyes. He had tools all over the foyer carpet; curlings of sawdust beneath the door where he was drilling into its edge. "Now you realize you can't just pull the door shut with this lock. You got to turn the key, otherwise it's not locked at all."

"I understand that. What concerns me is that nobody should be able to get in when it's locked. If I leave it unlocked it's my own stupidity."

"Sure. Well, there ain't no lock in the world that's sure proof against an experienced pickman, but there ain't many of them around and they usually don't go for buildings like this one. Where you get trouble with them's over on the East Side mostly – Fifth along the park, the East Sixties, Sutton Place, like that. I got one place I put three locks on their front door, most expensive locks you can buy, but didn't stop some pickman from getting in the day after he read in the papers about these folks sailing to Europe. Stripped the place clean."

The locksmith scraped sawdust out of the hole he had cut and began to fit an enormous device into it. "It sure don't pay to tell the newspapers you're going away," he said. "Listen, you wasn't planning to sell any valuables, are you?"

"Why?"

"If you do, don't put your name and address in the ad. That's an engraved invitation to thieves."

"I hadn't thought of that."

"Listen, there's plenty of things you can do to make it harder on these guys. Most people just leave one little light on when they go out – that's stupid. Every burglar in the world knows that leave-the-light-on routine. What I always tell my clients, when you go out for the evening or to the office for the day or whatever, leave two-three lights on and turn your radio on so a guy can hear it if he's standing outside your door. And there's another thing – the middle of the hot summer days, these dope addicts go along the street lookin' up at all the apartment house windows. They see an air-conditioner sticking out a window that's not turned on and dripping, they know nobody's home. It don't cost that much electricity to leave a few lights on and run your air conditioner on low when you ain't home, and leave the radio on. Cheap insurance. I always call it."

"I'll keep it in mind."

He hadn't skied since 1968, and then only a few timorous times, but in his dream he was skiing down a long white slope – faster and ever faster, and then the slope grew steeper and he could not turn, the cold wind scissored his ears, the skis whispered under him with terrifying sluicing speed, and the hill kept tilting downward and he could not turn.

He awoke with chilled feet and lay in bed listening to the garbage trucks and watching shards of dim light flash through the blinds. Out there they were killing people. There was nothing to think about but that; and nothing to do but think about it in the insomniac night.

His feet were cold and yet the room was filled with a dense stale heat and the thick-tongued smell of bad sleep. He got up and switched on the air conditioner, went to the refrigerator and poured a glass of milk and brought it back to the nightstand by the bed. Now over the chill drumming whisper of the air conditioner he heard the swishing of cars in the street – it had started raining. His eyes dreamily tracked the wavering liquid light-movements on the ceiling; he heard the rain when a gust of wind blew it against the window. Unable to stand it any longer he got up again and took a pair of wool socks from the drawer, put them on and got back into bed, pulling the covers up neatly over him. The edge of the sheet dragged the glass of milk over and spilled it to the carpet. He cursed at the top of his lungs; slammed out of bed and went to get the sponge and paper towels.

It was no good trying to sleep any more. Half-past two in the morning. He reached for a book but couldn't focus his eyes on the print; put it away and switched off the light and sat up in bed in the dark, sweating, staring.

Even in the darkness – perhaps especially in the darkness – the room had snaggy edges where memories clung. *I ought to give up the apartment, move somewhere.* Maybe move into one of those residential hotels where you got daily maid service.

The hell, he thought, *the only sane thing to do is move out of the city.* Get an efficiency in one of those highrises across the Hudson on the Palisades, or maybe even a cottage in Jersey or Orange County. Not Long Island,

he thought; he couldn't stand Long Island. But somewhere out of the city – out of this madness.

*That's wrong. That's giving in to them. I'm not run-
ning away. Stay and fight.*

Fight how?

The mind wove ridiculous fantasies in the middle of
the night. Feeling like an ass he got a glass of water,
washed down a sleeping pill, set the alarm and went
back to bed.

"Damn it, Lieutenant, haven't you got anywhere at
all?"

"We're doing everything we can, Mr. Benjamin.
We've picked up several people for questioning."

"That's not enough!"

"Look I know how you feel, sir, but we're doing everything we know how to do. We've assigned several
extra men to the case. Some of the best detectives on the
force. I don't know what else I could tell you."

"You could tell me you've nailed the bastards."

"I could, yes sir, but it wouldn't be true."

"The trail's getting colder all the time, Lieutenant."

"I know that sir."

"Damn it I want results!"

But the haranguing gave him no satisfaction and after
he hung up the phone he sat cracking his knuckles and
looking for someone to hit.

Lunch in Schrafft's – single tables occupied by little
old ladies in prim hats. *We are all dressing for dinner
in the jungle.* He remembered a year or so ago in
the same restaurant – lunching with Sam Kreutzer that
day – he'd sat and watched an elderly woman alone at
a table suddenly hurl water tumblers and silverware at

the wall mirror. He had been shocked. If it happened today he would regard it as predictably logical behavior. Everybody lived like a character in a one-act play that nobody understood; getting by from one moment to the next was like trying to hold onto your hat in a gusty wind.

He returned to the office after lunch and spent an hour deliberating over the Amercon papers George Eng had delivered two days earlier. Steeping himself in figures and processes so he would be ready for the trip out West at the end of next week.

At half-past three he phoned Jack's office but Jack was in court. He tried again just before five and caught him in. "How is she?"

"Rotten."

His scalp contracted. "What's happened?"

"Nothing sudden. It's hard to describe – it's like watching someone sink into quicksand and knowing there isn't a damn thing you can do about it."

"She's just not responding?"

"The doctor's starting to talk about shock treatments. Insulin shock, not electric."

He was tired, suddenly; his swollen eyes took longer to blink. Coming on top of the rest it was just too much to expect a man to bear.

Jack was saying, ". . . form of amnesiac catatonia. She looks at things and evidently she sees them, she recognizes you when you walk into the room, but it's as if there's no *emotional* reaction. As if she observes everything without any associations. You can turn her around and give her a push and she'll walk across the room as obediently as a wind-up toy. She eats by herself if you put the food in front of her but she doesn't seem to care what it is. She ate a whole plate full of calves

90

liver last night and you know how she detests the stuff. She didn't even seem to notice. It's as if there's some kind of short-circuit somewhere between the taste-buds and the brain, or between the eyes and the brain. When I go in to see her she knows who I am, but she doesn't *recognize* me – not in the sense of relating me to herself."

He listened to Jack's words and feeling almost burst his throat.

After he hung up, Dundee came into the office. Took one look at his face and said in alarm, "Paul?"

"There's nothing to talk about, Bill. Not right now."

He left the building and walked through Grand Central to the subway steps, moving with a heavy deliberation in his tread. Walked down to the platform and waited for the crosstown Shuttle. The tunnel was hot and crowded, stinking of stale air and urine and soot. Grease-sweaty people jostled angrily along the brink of the platform. He had never actually seen anyone pushed off onto the tracks, but he knew it happened. Whole rows of people, jammed together, leaning vertiginously out over the concrete lip to peer down the tracks in search of approaching headlight beams.

The trains were running slow today; when the next one came in he had to squeeze into it and suck in his belly against the closing doors. It was impossible to breathe. He flattened his hand over his wallet pocket and kept it there for the duration of the brief ride to Times Square. A black fist clutched the steel overhead strap by his cheek. Scarred knuckles, pink cuticles. He looked over his shoulder and for a moment he could have sworn it was the same man in the cowboy hat who'd been standing on his corner a few nights ago, staring at him, smiling. After a moment he realized

91

it wasn't the same face. *Getting paranoid for sure*, he thought.

For some indeterminate reason the Broadway Express was less crowded; usually it was packed more thickly than the Shuttle. But he found a seat and sat with his legs close together and his elbows tight against his abdomen, squeezed between two women. One of them had a sickening load of garlic on her breath; he averted his face and breathed as shallowly as he could. The train lurched and swayed on its worn-out rails. Motes of filth hung visibly in the air. Some of the ceiling lights had blown out; half the car was in gloom. He found he was looking from face to face along the rows of crowded passengers, resentfully scanning them for signs of redeeming worth: if you wanted to do something about overpopulation this was the place to start. He made a head-count and discovered that of the fifty-eight faces he could see, seven appeared to belong to people who had a right to survive. The rest were fodder.

I should have been a Nazi. A shrieking of brake shoes; the train bucked to a halt. He dived out of the car onto the Seventy-second Street platform and followed the crowd to the narrow stairs. The funnel blocked everything and the crowd stood and milled like bees around a hive; it was an inexcusable time before he was on the stairs. They were cattle being prodded up a chute. Human cattle most of them: you could see in their faces and bodies they didn't deserve life, they had nothing to contribute except the smelly unimaginative existences of their wretched carcasses. They had never read a book, created a phrase, looked at a budding flower and really seen it. All they did was get in your way. Their lives were unending litanies of anger and frustration and complaint; they whined their way from cradle to grave. What good were they to anyone? Exterminate them.

He battled his way through to the turnstile, using his elbows with indiscriminate discourtesy; rushed outside onto the concrete island and stood there getting his breath while the light changed.

He cried at the corny sad dramas on television; he knew every commercial by heart. At half-past nine in the middle of a program an announcer said, "...will continue following station identification," and he stormed across the room and switched the set off.

After he thought, *not "following." Where the hell did those imbeciles go to school? It's* after *station identification.*

I am strung out. Need something. A woman?

No whores. With a whore it would be a mockery. Maybe a woman: a compatible stranger. In the city they were supposed to be easy to find, although he had never tried.

A bar, he thought. Wasn't that where lonely people were supposed to go? But he never went to bars alone. He had never been able to understand people who did.

Still it was better than rotting in this caged isolation. He knotted his tie and shouldered into his jacket and went out.

10

He sat on the bar stool with his heels hooked on its chrome ring, holding his knees together stiffly to avoid touching the man next to him. "God damn right I'm a bigot," the man was saying. "I'm a better man than any nigger I ever met."

He was big without much black hair left on top of his skull; a man who worked with his hands and probably with his back. Grease-smeared gray trousers, a flannel shirt with the sleeves rolled up to the elbows and hair crawling on his arms. If he had tattoos they weren't on his forearms but he looked the type.

There had been a black couple in the place: well-dressed in flaunt-it-baby outfits, the leather and the bright colours and the Afro hair. When they had left the bar the big man had turned without preamble and started talking to Paul: "Fucking spades come in here like they own the place. You work for a living, right? *I* work for a living, my kids go to crummy schools, they don't get to no summer camps – the fucking politicians ain't worried about *my* kids, all they worry about is the fucking spades get the summer camps and the schools. You know how many million niggers we got on welfare you and me are supporting with our taxes? Here I read in the paper this morning some fat welfare niggers put on a demonstration march down at City Hall, you read about that?"

"No. . . ."

"Demanding – not asking, *demanding* a fucking allowance for Christmas presents for their fucking bastard kids. Anybody ever send *you* a Christmas allowance for your kids? Christ I *work* for a living and I don't get no fancy presents for my kids, I can't afford it, they're lucky they get a couple toy cars and a new outfit of clothes to go to school in. And everybody always bleeding about the fucking spades, Jesus H. Christ if I hear that three-hundred-years-slavery number one more time I'm gonna strangle the son of a bitch that pitches it at me, I swear to God. They don't just want to move in next door to you, they want to burn your fucking *house* down, and what happens? Some nigger-lovin' son of a bitch says we got to pay more taxes and give the spades more of *our* hard-earned money and let them take our jobs away from us because that way maybe they'll be nice to us and they won't burn my house down after all. Well I'm tellin' you –" he leveled a finger at Paul "– it's all a crock of shit and any spade bastard tries to toss a brick through *my* window is gonna get his nigger hide blown in a lot of pieces. I got a legal registered shotgun by my front door and I see any black son of a bitch prowling around my place he's gonna get killed first and asked questions later. You got to get tough with the bastards, it's the only thing they understand."

A month ago Paul would have tried to find a way to show him it wasn't that simple, wasn't that cut-and-dried. Now he was no longer sure the man wasn't right. Permissive societies were like permissive parents: they produced hellish children.

He thought bitterly, *A man ought to be able to keep a few illusions. . . .*

Finally the man looked at the revolving clock above the bar; drained his beer and left. Paul ordered his third gin and tonic and sat rotating the glass between his palms, seeking something to look at. There were five booths along the wall behind him; two were occupied by couples who seemed to be arguing in tense whispers. A big woman sat alone in the front booth watching the street; now and then she would turn to signal the bartender and Paul had glimpses of a puffy face, too old and ravaged to go with the blonde-dyed hair. She kept getting up and putting coins in the jukebox by the door; the room vibrated and Paul wondered why saloon jukeboxes inevitably emphasized the heavy brass thumpings.

All I'd have to do is go over and say, 'Mind if I sit down?'

He didn't; he knew he wouldn't.

Once she even stopped on her way back to the booth and stared straight at him. He dropped his eyes and had an impression of her shrugging and turning away. When he looked up she was sliding into the booth, buttocks writhing, the cotton dress stretched tight across her full-nesses.

The bartender refilled his glass and Paul tried to strike up a conversation but the bartender wasn't the talkative kind, or possibly something had put him in a mood. There were five or six men clustered at the far end of the bar, half-watching the television ball game, talking among themselves with the easy familiarity of long acquaintance; probably neighborhood shop managers – dry cleaners, shoe repairmen, delicatessen types – and they didn't look as if they would welcome a stranger's intrusion.

He paid the tab and got off the stool and swallowed the fourth drink too fast, and felt the effect of it a moment after he hit the sidewalk. The traffic on Broadway seemed to be moving too fast for his eyes to track. He had to make an effort to walk without weaving. At the corner of Seventy-fourth Street he decided to cut across town on the side street because he didn't want all the people on Seventy-second to see him in this condition.

He was several yards into the block before the fear hit him. There was no one in sight down the entire length of the street; the shadows were sinister and the heavily massed buildings threw dangerous projections into the street – steps, awnings, parked vans: killers could be hiding behind them, or in the narrow service alleys. . . .

He remembered the other night, his terror crossing the East Side in the Forties; he drew himself up. *It's about time to quit getting railroaded into panic.* He walked forward with quicker steps; but his hand in his pocket closed around the sock-wrapped roll of coins and his bowels were knotted and it was no good pretending the soul-sucking darkness wasn't alive with terrors. The beat of his heart was as loud as the echoes of his heels on the concrete.

At first he did not hear the movement behind him.

In the corner of his vision an apparitious shape. He did not stop or turn; he kept moving and kept his eyes straight ahead in the insane hope that if he pretended it wasn't there it would go away. He was walking fast but he couldn't betray his fear by breaking into a run. Life was suddenly all he had, and all he wanted. Maybe it was his imagination after all – maybe there was no one, only the echoes of his own steps, his own shadow moving across a stucco wall? Yet he did not look back, he could not. Half the long block yet to traverse, the streetlamp throwing a pool of light that made the shadows deeper.

"Hey hold it motherfucker."

The voice like a blade against his spine.

Close enough to touch. Right there behind him.

"Hold up. Turn around, honkie."

I'm hearing things it's my imagination.

He stood bolt still in his tracks, shoulders tensed against awaited violence.

"*Motherfucker I said turn around.*" It was quiet, tense – high-pitched, a little crack in it. An adolescent voice, a tone of raging bravado – *bravado to mask fear.*

Petrified. But: *My God he's as scared as I am!*

And as Paul turned slowly to face his fear he heard the snap-blade knife open with a click and something inside him exploded like a brilliant deafening burst of discovery:

Anger.

A furious physical rage.

The adrenalin was shooting through him and he felt the heat exploding through his head; even as he came around and the attacker came in view Paul was lifting the roll of coins from his pocket, whipping his arm up overhead, stretching to smite this enemy the mightiest blow his inflamed muscles could deliver. . . .

He caught the fragmentary race of reflected lamplight along the moving blade of the knife; saw it but did not register it, all he knew was the target and the weight of the kosh swinging from his hand, swinging down toward that dark narrow weaving skull. . . . And he heard the enormous bellow that thundered from his own chest, the bestial cry of berserk assault. . . .

. . . And the kid with the knife was falling back in panic, dodging, arms whipping up over his head; wheeling, scrabbling, getting his balance, digging in his toes – *running.* . . .

The savage downswing found no target and Paul stayed his hand before the roll of coins could smash his

98

own knee but it made him lose his balance and he broke his fall with a palm – got one knee under him and knelt there watching the kid who wasn't more than half his size or weight, the kid running away up the street, flitting into an alley, instantly absorbed into the city as if he hadn't been there at all.

The street was empty and he got to his feet but it hit him then, the reaction, and he began to shake so badly he had to reach for the railing of a brownstone's front steps. He hung onto it and pivoted on his hands, collapsing in a circle until he was seated on the third step from the bottom. Hot flushes and chills prickled his flesh, his vision spun, and a surge of uncontainable exultation lifted his voice to a high call of joy:

"Haaaaaaaaaaaaaa!"

11

Trying to conceal the fact that he was breathing hard he gave the doorman an idiot grin and crossed the lobby on drunken legs and stood in the elevator until its doors closed; he slid to the floor and sat there until they opened, crawled out and let himself into the apartment with vomit pain convulsing his stomach. Leaned over the kitchen sink and catted up everything.

He rinsed his mouth and threw up again and rinsed again. Hung in the sink with painful dry heaves until it subsided. Sweating, scalp prickling, he made it to the living-room couch and lay down weak and wet. Felt himself pass out.

... When the grinding of the garbage trucks awakened him his first thought was *I wasn't nearly that drunk.* Then he remembered it all.

But he hadn't slept as well in weeks: when he looked at the time it was half-past eight. It couldn't have been much later than eleven when he'd come home. There was no hangover; he hadn't felt this well since – he couldn't remember when.

In the subway he got out of his seat to give it to an old woman; he smiled at her look of surprise. When he left the Express at Times Square and stood on the Shuttle platform waiting for the crosstown train he realized he was still smiling and he wiped it off his face with an effort; it was occurring to him that he was experiencing all the symptoms of a sexual release and that worried him.

All morning in the office he tried to keep his attention on the figures and notes in front of him but last night kept getting in the way. Why hadn't he called the police? Well, he hadn't really seen the kid's face, he probably wouldn't know it if he saw him again; and anyhow judging by experience the cops wouldn't accomplish a damned thing and he'd only have to waste hours telling the story half a dozen times, signing statements, looking through mugshots. *A waste of my time and theirs.*

But that wasn't really it; those were rationalizations and he knew that much.

Rationalizations for what?

He still didn't have the answer when Dundee came in and took him to lunch at the Pen and Pencil.

"Christ, you're eating like you haven't seen a square meal in a month."

"Just getting my appetite back," Paul said.

"Well that's a good thing. Or maybe it isn't. You've lost some weight – it looks good on you. Wish I could. I've spent the last two years on cottage cheese lunches and no potatoes. Haven't dropped a pound. You're lucky – you're just about ready to have your clothes taken in."

He hadn't even noticed.

Dundee said, "I guess this Amercon deal's put you back on your feed, hey? That's a good break, getting that thing tossed your way. I kind of envy you."

It made him feel guilty because by now he ought to be on top of the case, he ought to have every figure and fact on the tip of his tongue; he felt like a schoolboy who'd daydreamed his way through his homework.

That afternoon he made a great effort to buckle down to it. But when he left the office he realized how little of it had penetrated. His mind was too crowded to admit digits and decimals; they simply didn't matter enough any more.

Now damn it straighten up. It's your job you're risking.

He had a hamburger in Squire's coffee shop on the corner and afterward he still felt hungry but he didn't order dessert. He kept remembering Dundee's compliments. He walked home and weighed himself and discovered he was down to 175 for the first time in ten years. The skin hung a little loose on his face and belly but he could feel his ribs. He decided to join a health club and start doing daily workouts in a gym – there was one in the Shelton Hotel a few blocks up from the office, three or four of the accountants went there every day. *You've got to be in shape.*

In shape for what?

He thumbed through the *Post* and his eyes paused on an ad for a karate school and that put everything together; he said aloud, "You're nuts," and threw the newspaper across the room. But ten minutes later he found he was thinking about going back to that same bar on Broadway and he was now alert enough to realize why: it wasn't the bar he was thinking of, it was the walk home.

It brought him bolt upright in the chair. He wanted that kid to try it again.

He got up and began to pace back and forth through the apartment. "Now take – take it easy. For God's sake don't get carried away."

He had started talking to himself sometime in the past week or two; he realized he was going to have to watch that or one day he'd catch himself doing it on the street. At least he began to feel he understood the people you saw doing it on the sidewalks – walking along by themselves having loud animated arguments with imaginary companions, complete with gestures and positive emphatic answers to questions no one in earshot had asked. You passed them all the time and you edged away from them and refused to meet their eyes. But now he was beginning to know them.

"Easy," he muttered again. He knew he was getting as filled up with inflated bravado as that kid had been last night. One accidental victory and he had become as smug as an armed guard in a prison for the blind.

You were lucky. That kid was scared. Most of them aren't scared. Most of them are killers. And he remembered the rage that had flooded his tissues, overcoming every inhibition: if he'd pulled that on a veteran street mugger he'd have been dead now, or in an emergency ward bleeding from sixteen slices.

He'd had twenty-four hours of euphoria; it was time to be realistic. It wasn't his courage that had saved him; it wasn't even the poor weapon, the roll of quarters; it was luck, the kid's fear. Maybe it had been the kid's first attempt.

But what if it had been a hardened thug? Or a pack of them?

His toe caught the discarded *Post* and he bent to pick it up and take it to the wastebasket. The ad for the karate school returned to mind, and the resolve to take up gym workouts. That's no answer, he thought. It took years to develop hand-to-hand skills; he'd heard enough cocktail party chitchat to know that much. Two, three years and you might be good enough to earn yourself a black belt or whatever they called it. But what good was that against a killer with a gun, or six kids with knives?

He turned on the TV and sat down to watch it. One

of the local unaffiliated channels; a rerun of a horse-opera series the networks had cancelled years ago. Cowboys picking on sodbusters and a drifting hero standing up for the farmers against the gunslingers. He watched it for an hour. It was easy to see why Westerns were always popular and he was amazed he hadn't understood it before. It was human history. As far back as you wanted to go, there were always men who tilled the soil and there were always men on horseback who wanted to exploit them and take everything away from them, and the hero of every myth was the hero who defended the farmers against the raiders on horseback, and the constant contradiction was that the hero himself was always a man on horseback. The bad guys might be Romans or Huns or Mongols or cattlemen, it was always the same, and the good guy was always a reformed Roman or Hun or Mongol or cattleman; either that or a farmer who learned to fight like a Hun. Organize the farmers into imitation Huns and beat the real Huns at their own game.

There had never been a successful TV series about a Gandhi; there were only cowboys and private eyes. Robin Hood was a gunslinger in a white hat and the Sheriff of Nottingham was a gunslinger in a black hat and there was no difference between ways of fighting, it was only a question of who fought best. And most of the time the theme was the same: you had to be willing to stand and fight for your own or the gunslingers on horseback would take it away from you.

You had to be willing to fight. That was what the hero always taught the sodbusters.

We have been teaching ourselves that lesson for thousands of years and we haven't learned it yet.

He was beginning to learn it. It was what made him

want to return to the dark street and find the scared kid
with the knife.

I feel like a fight. So help me I feel like a fight.

But you had to use your head. Your guts said one
thing, your head said another, and your guts usually
won; but still you had to use your head, and the head
made it crystal clear it wasn't enough to let blind rage
sweep over you – because next time it wouldn't be a
scared kid, next time it would be a hoodlum with a gun,
and lunatic rage was no match for a gun. The only match
for a gun was a gun of your own.

12

Jack handed him the drink. "Prosit."

He carried it to the couch and sat. "You think she's really feeling better then."

"Dr. Metz said he was encouraged."

"They're not going to use insulin shock?"

"He wants to hold off a little while and see if she comes out of it by herself." Jack pulled a chair out and sat down with elbows on the dining table. A pack of cards sat neatly squared on the table; he had probably worn them out playing solitaire. He looked haggard. "I guess there's nothing else to do. Just wait and see. Christ but it doesn't get any easier, Pop."

"I know."

"Watching her just sit on the edge of the bed like that, picking fluff. . . ."

"I'd like to see her."

"Believe me it wouldn't make you feel any better."

"They're excluding me from things, these doctors. There's no sane reason for it."

"Her reasons aren't sane right now, Pop. But I'll ask Metz, I'll see what I can do."

Paul swallowed a sulphurous comment. He knew if he kicked up enough of a fuss they would let him see her but was there sufficient point to it? Yet in the meantime they were acting as though he were a poor relation with some sort of communicable disease. He was insulted. But Jack seemed too vulnerable; his eyes now pleaded with Paul not to ask him any more questions to which he didn't have answers.

He set down his glass empty. He was doing a lot of fast drinking lately. Well it was understandable, wasn't it; he wasn't going to start worrying about *that*, there were too many other things to think about right now.

He knew what he wanted to ask Jack; he wasn't sure how to lead into it. Finally he said, "I was attacked the other night."

"You *what*?"

"A kid on the street. He had a knife. I suppose he wanted money."

"You suppose? You don't know?"

"I scared him off." He took pride in saying it.

Jack gaped at him. "You scared...." It was unconsciously a comic reaction; Paul had to force himself not to smile. "For God's sake Pop."

"Well I suppose I was lucky. A Negro kid, probably not more than twelve or thirteen. He had a knife but he didn't seem to know what to do with it. I yelled at him and started to hit him – I was mad clear through, you can understand that. I didn't stop to think. I suppose if he'd known what he was doing I'd have been sliced to ribbons."

"Jesus," Jack whispered. He stared, not blinking.

"Anyhow the next thing I knew he was running away."

"But – where'd this happen?"

"Right around the corner from the apartment. Seventy-fourth between West End and Amsterdam."

"Late at night?"

"Not very late, no. It must have been around eleven."

"What did the police do?"

"Nothing. I didn't call them."

"Christ, Pop, you should have –"

"Oh, to hell with that, I didn't get much of a look at

107

him. What could they have done? By the time I got any-where near a phone that kid was six blocks away."

"A junkie?"

"I have no idea. I guess it's likely, isn't it?"

"Most of them are."

"Well the truth is I was angry. I was madder than I've ever been in my life."

"So you just started hitting the kid? Jesus that's a ballsy thing to do. . . ."

"Well I wasn't thinking straight, obviously. I never landed a blow on him – he bolted and ran the minute I started to swing at him. I had a roll of coins in my hand, I suppose he mistook it for something more lethal." Paul leaned forward for emphasis. "But suppose it hadn't been a mixed-up kid? Suppose it had been a real tough?"

"You're leading up to something, aren't you?"

"Jack, they're on every street. They jump people at five o'clock in broad daylight. They hold up subway cars as if they were stagecoaches. All right, it happens all the time, but what are we supposed to do about it? What am *I* supposed to do about it? Throw my arms up over my head and yell for help?"

"Well, usually if you just keep calm and give them the money they'll leave you alone, Pop. All most of them want is money. There aren't too many of them like the ones who killed Mom."

"So we're just supposed to turn the other cheek, are we?" He stood up abruptly. It made Jack's head skew back. Paul said, "Damn it that's not enough for me. Not any more. The next time one of the bastards accosts me in the street I want to have a gun in my pocket."

"Now wait a minute –"

"What for? Wait until the next mugger jumps me and decides to stick a knife in me?" He was on his feet and it

108

felt stagey, foolish; for something to do he picked up his empty glass and carried it to the bar cabinet. He talked while he mixed a drink.

"Jack, you're in with all the criminal lawyers, you know people in the District Attorney's office. I want a pistol permit."

"It's not that easy, Pop."

"I read somewhere there are half a million New Yorkers who own firearms."

"Sure. Shotguns for hunting, mostly. The rest of them are mainly war souvenirs and rifles. A certain number of people own guns illegally, of course, but that's a violation of the Sullivan Law – you could get sent up for twenty years for carrying a gun without a ticket."

"What about all the storekeepers who keep pistols under their cash registers? What about them?"

"Pop, it's a different kind of ticket. The Bureau of Licenses issues pistol permits in two categories – premises and carry. You could probably get a premises permit if you wanted to stow a captured German Luger in your apartment or something like that, but that's totally different from getting a permit to carry a concealed weapon on the streets."

"Then what about all these gangsters who've got licenses to carry guns?"

"It's a corrupt city, Pop, we all know that. If you've got ten or twelve thousand dollars to spare to grease certain people, you can get a concealed-pistol permit. It's not fair but it's the way things work. It's an outrageous price, but the Mafia can afford it and it protects them from the inconvenience of being run in on a weapons charge. But I never heard of an ordinary law-abiding citizen willing to spend that kind of money on a gun. Even if you did it would make them suspect you were some sort of criminal. They'd start bugging your apartment and your phone and you'd live your whole life under surveillance. Is that what you want?"

"All I want is the machinery to defend myself."

"Have you thought of moving out of the city?"

"Have you?" he countered.

"God damn right I have. As soon as Carol's on her feet we're getting out of this hell hole. I've already started reading the real estate ads. You ought to do the same thing, Pop."

"No. I thought about it. I won't do it."

"Why?"

"I was born here. I've spent my whole life here. I tried living in the suburbs. It didn't work. I'm too old to change, I know my limitations."

"But things aren't the same as they were then, Pop. It used to be a place where you could live."

It was a bilious tone he had never heard from Jack before; but he shook his head. "I won't run. I just won't."

"Why the hell not? What's keeping you here?"

It was too hard to explain. He wasn't going to allow himself to be driven from his home by a pack of savages who weren't fit to wipe his shoes. But how did you say that aloud without making it sound like a corny line from an old cowboy movie?

What he said was, "Then you won't help me get a gun permit?"

"I can't, Pop. I haven't got that kind of clout."

"And I get the feeling from you that even if you did, you wouldn't use it. You don't approve of the whole idea."

"No. I don't. I don't think adding to the arsenal on the streets is going to help calm things down any."

110

"It's too late to calm anything down," he said. "It's about time we revived our self-respect, don't you think? Nobody should have to walk down a public street half-paralyzed by fear that somebody could come leaping out of any doorway with a switchblade knife. Human beings just shouldn't have to live that way."

"And you think having a loaded gun in your pocket would give you back your self-respect and make you feel ten feet tall. Is that it?"

Now who sounds like bad dialogue from an old movie? But he didn't laugh; Jack had neither the imagination nor the sense of humor to appreciate it.

Jack said, "You're kidding yourself, Pop. Have you ever even handled a pistol in your entire life?"

"I was in the Army."

"All right so you were in the Army. You were a clerk-typist, not a combat infantryman."

"We still had to qualify on the range. I've handled guns."

"Rifles. It's hardly the same thing. A handgun's a very tricky job to handle, Pop. People who don't know them very well are always blowing holes in their own knees. And what happens if you're accosted by another man with a gun? What happens when he sees your gun? Christ you'd get your ass blown off." Jack spread his hands and ducked his chin toward his chest. "Look, you'd better forget the whole idea. Guns aren't panaceas, Pop. Bullets never answered any questions."

"I don't want to ask questions. I want to protect my life. What is it in this day and age that makes that simple desire so incredibly immoral and wrong?"

He gave in because Jack wasn't going to; there wasn't much point prolonging it. He knew all the arguments to

111

which Jack would resort; he had used them all himself, in the past. And to keep pressing the point would make Jack suspicious that perhaps Paul had something more than self-defense in mind.

On the way home he asked himself exactly what he did have in mind.

Revenge, he thought. It lay curled in the back of his mind like a poison snake.

But it was a meaningless fantasy, really. The police had got nowhere; they would never get anywhere. Esther's killers were free and there wasn't a chance in the world of anyone's ever finding them. Sooner or later they would be arrested for something, but it wasn't likely this crime would ever be pinned on them. No one knew who they were and there was no way to find out. So it didn't matter, that way, whether or not you went armed in the streets; you'd never have a chance to take a shot at them. You wouldn't know them if you walked right into them.

Still, he *had* wanted a gun. Jack's advice was simple to disregard, but he did know the facts; it was a keen disappointment to find out how impossible it was to obtain a pistol license.

It was dark when he came up out of the subway. The fear settled in his bowels again when he walked the single crosstown block to West End Avenue. No one accosted him, he reached the apartment without incident; but he was covered with oily sweat.

I just don't want to feel like this, he thought. *Is it so much to ask?*

13

A phone rang, closer to the bed than it should have been. He blinked. The surroundings were unfamiliar and with momentary disorientation he rolled over, saw the phone and listened to it ring again. His arm reached it and tipped it off and he heard a weary female voice whine, "Seven-thirty, sir, you left a wake-up call."

The motel. The Arizona heat just beyond the whispering air conditioner.

He ate breakfast quickly in the coffee shop and went back to the diagonally ruled parking slot in front of his room where the rent-a-car sat; the sun shot painful reflections off its chrome, the dry heat was already building toward another suffocating noon. He climbed in and started the car. The steering wheel had sun on it; its rim was almost too hot to touch. He switched on the air conditioner but the engine hadn't smoothed out and it stalled. He cursed mildly and spent a while grinding the starter before it caught again.

He had always kept his driver's license up even though he hadn't owned a car in two decades nor driven one in several years. He still felt uncomfortable behind the wheel after nearly a week on these boulevards and freeways; it was a different style of driving out here, philosophically different from the kind of dodging and diving you got used to in city taxis. There was just as much aggression here but it was a high-speed kind and they came at you blinding fast from long distances away. Tucson had a main boulevard actually named Speedway; it had a green mall down the centre, palm trees and lawn, several lines on either side – the street itself was as wide as a New York city block and the drivers seemed to have cross-country racing in mind. Miles of it were lined with sportscar showrooms and speed shops and car-washes and gas stations. Everything glittered too much; even with sunglasses he had to squint.

Williamson had told him about the series of grisly murders. They were scared here too. No place was immune any more. You thought of muggings and murders as dark city things – as if wide boulevards and low roof-tops and a brass desert sun would inhibit them – but the crime rate was alarming here too and Williamson carried a revolver in the glove-compartment of his Cadillac.

Paul envied him. Two days ago he had asked where Williamson had got the gun – how he'd got a license for it.

"Well, you don't need a license to buy one. You've got to register it of course – the federal act – but they can't refuse to sell you a gun as long as you can prove you haven't got a criminal record. Technically you're not supposed to carry a concealed weapon, and the cops enforce that if they catch you with a gun in your pocket, but I never heard of anybody getting arrested for carrying a piece in his car or keeping a gun in his house. Course you can get a concealed-weapon permit from the local cops if you really want one. Not like back East, thank God."

They were all right-wing down here, it was Goldwater country. He hadn't lost his contempt for their attitudes on almost everything. They supported free enterprise for the poor and socialized subsidies for the rich. They insisted on your right to die if you didn't have enough money to afford expensive private medical treatment.

114

They saw Communists behind every bush and wanted to drop Nukes on Moscow and Peking. You had a right to good transportation if you had the price of a Cadillac; Tucson had no public transportation to speak of.

But they had a hard-nosed fundamentalist attitude toward crime and he knew now they were right about that.

Jainchill's head offices occupied the top three floors of a very new high-rise building near the foothills of the mountains that loomed over the city. The building was all plastic and glass, it had all the warmth of a digital computer. He put the car in the vast parking lot and went into the lobby and felt the blast of chilled air hit him like an arctic wind after the heat outside. He pressed the elevator's depressed plastic square and watched it light up.

They had assigned a conference room to him. The long table was littered with ledgers and documents. He spent the morning alone with columns of figures; at noon he left the building and drove to the restaurant to meet George Eng for lunch. On the way he got caught in a little knot of traffic; a fool blocked his way, one of those uncertain drivers who crept through the intersection and inevitably put on a burst and squirted through the traffic just as it turned amber, leaving Paul stranded at the stoplight. He looked at his watch and chafed.

On the corner beside him stood a small shop with fishing tackle and bicycles and guns in the display window. Hunting rifles, shotguns, more varieties of handguns than he had ever thought existed. He stared at them

A horn blared behind him. The light had changed. He drove across the intersection, craning his neck to find the street signs. He couldn't see them. The idiot behind him blatted again and he drove on, never having found

115

out what cross-street it had been. But he knew he was on Fourth Avenue; he'd be able to find it again. He dipped down into the sudden dimness of the railroad underpass and when he emerged from it he began to look for a place to park.

"The shrimp's pretty good here. It's Guaymas shrimp, they fly it up here fresh."

"I bow to the wisdom of the East," Paul said and closed the menu.

George Eng smiled at the little joke and gave the order to the hovering waiter. When they had been left alone at the table with their drinks he said to Paul, "How's it going?"

"Steady and tiresome. I haven't found anything shocking."

"Kind of hoped you wouldn't." George Eng was fleshy around the face and his movements were those of a heavy man but he was not overweight. Paul had only met him within the past year; he assumed Eng had done a good deal of dieting in the recent past but hadn't yet got used to being slender. He had a thin feathering of dark hair and a self-conscious Fu Manchu moustache that lent his Oriental features a sinister appearance. He had been born in Hawaii into a wealthy family; he had no discernible accent. He dressed with conservative care and had expensive tastes; he was a good businessman with a quick decisive mind. Paul had met him only at business affairs and gatherings associated with business – cocktail parties, luncheons. He knew nothing about the man outside of that context; Eng was a private person, he didn't open up. It had been months before Paul had screwed up the nerve to crack mild and inoffensive Oriental jokes at him, and he'd only started because it

116

had become evident that Eng expected it and enjoyed it. He played the role of Chinese man-of-mystery with deliberate intent.

It was the sort of restaurant that did most of its business at the noon hour and attracted a business-lunch clientele of the kind that didn't stint on expense accounts. The drinks were generous, the menu straightforward but served with a proper elegance, and the tables were separated by pillars and rubber plants and discreet distances. The lighting was recessed and indirect but you didn't have to strain your eyes to read your partner's expressions.

"All right," George Eng said, "let's wheel and deal. You've been at it all week. What can you tell me?"

"It's pretty much what we expected. Nothing alarming. Naturally they've done everything they can to put the company in the best light – they've seen you coming. for quite some time."

"In a way we did that on purpose. Wanted to see how much skulduggery their management was willing to indulge in. We've given them ample opportunity to show their true colors, don't you think?"

"I'd say so, yes."

"And what *are* their true colors?"

"I'd call it pale gray," Paul said. "You've already seen the routine posting-and-footing audit; that was done back in New York with electronic data-processing. We already knew they'd done some mild fiddling with their earned surplus and net working capital and other vagaries like that."

"You're suggesting I needn't be surprised to find they've carried that policy through to the rest of the company."

Paul nodded. "I didn't think it would put you off."

"What specifically are we talking about now?"

"I've found half a dozen points you can use for leverage, I think. For instance they've tried to show a sharp increase in assets by reporting the company's subsidiaries at book value instead of original cost."

Eng made a face. "That's a little cheap. I'm disappointed in Jainchill."

"You can't really blame him for trying."

"I had a sneaking hope he'd be a little less obvious than that. What else?"

"Well, they've started amortizing their research costs over a five-year span. They only started doing that last year – before that they were absorbing them immediately in each fiscal year. Nothing dishonest about it, but it does paint a brighter picture. The only other thing of any consequence I've been able to find is a sharp increase, within the past eighteen months, in stock options to their executives."

"In lieu of cash bonuses, you mean."

"Yes. They used to pay cash bonuses almost exclusively."

"What do the stock options amount to?".

"I'm still working on those sheets. If I had to make a general projection I'd say it would be in the neighbourhood of four hundred thousand dollars."

Eng put a cigarette into a stubby silver holder and lit it with a jeweled lighter. "And of course those stock options aren't charged to income."

"No."

"Stock options," Eng muttered, "can turn out to be a long-run drain on per-share dividends. They could end up diluting their capitalization if they kept it up at that rate."

118

"Well, I'm sure they had no intention of keeping it up. They knew you were nosing around, there was a good chance of a take-over bid from Amercon – you'd have done the same thing, in their shoes."

"In effect, then, they've been paying bonuses to their own executives in the form of options on what they hope will be Amercon stocks."

"It amounts to that."

"That's a little blatant," Eng observed, "but if it's the worst they've tried to pull, I'm not going to lose any sleep over it. I was more concerned about the possibility that their cost system didn't reflect actual production costs, or that they might be saddled with big inventories of obsolete stock that they never bothered to write down or charge off. I've run into that several times – losses that should have been taken long ago, but somehow end up staying back in a warehouse somewhere with no liability accounts to cover them." His eyes suddenly whipped up to Paul's face. "But you haven't found anything like that."

"No. That's not to say it couldn't exist. I just haven't found any signs pointing that way. We won't know for sure until we've been over the inventory sheets for all their subsidiaries."

"How long do you expect that to take?"

"Depends on how detailed an audit you want. Jainchill's got five subsidiaries. He took over three of them within the past four years. Naturally at the time of the mergers he had audits done. Now either we can accept those figures or we can duplicate those audits ourselves."

"What would you recommend, Paul?"

"I'd be willing to accept his audits. It would cost you quite a bit of money and three or four months' time to dig back into all that stuff now. And don't forget, Jainchill didn't have a buyer for his own company sniffing around when he went into those mergers. He hired competent accountants and they did a thorough job of investigation for him before he moved in and took over these subsidiaries. He couldn't afford to do any less than that – he had to be sure he wasn't buying a pig in a poke. He was in the same position then that you're in now."

Eng speared a shrimp and sat with it half-raised over the plate. "Suppose we decide to accept those figures. How long will it take you to finish up the rest of your audit?"

"My end of it or the whole operation?"

"They should be finished in New York by the end of this coming week. I'm asking about your own work here."

"From the way things look right now, I'd say I should have everything I need here by the middle of the week. Say Wednesday evening. Then I'll need a few more days on the computers back in New York. Ten days from now ought to wrap up the whole thing."

Eng nodded. "Good. Then let's do it that way. My board of directors is anxious to get this merger rolling." The shrimp made the rest of the trip to his mouth and disappeared inside. "How do you like it out here?"

The sudden switch of tone and topic took him off guard. "Well – it's kind of hot."

Eng shrugged. "Everything's air conditioned. Half the year it's pleasant anyway – no snow, you never need an overcoat."

"So they tell me."

"I gather you don't like it much."

"I wouldn't say that. It's too difficult a life-style for

me, I suppose – I've spent my whole life in New York. I've nothing against it for other people. But it does remind me of the suburbs. Does that make any sense?"

"Yes. There's a small-town flavour to it even though there's half a million people here. I take it you must have tried the suburbs at one time."

Paul nodded, finished chewing, swallowed, reached for his napkin. "Some years ago. You need a certain kind of patience to live in a house and put up with all the mechanical things. Every time you want to buy a newspaper or a carton of milk you've got to get in a car and drive somewhere. It's all right for most people – I just never got in tune with it. And I always hated the idea of neighbors nosing around one another. In the city your neighbors don't bother you unless you make it clear you want them to."

"I'm a little surprised to hear you talk that way, after what happened."

"I like to think my wife would have understood."

Headlights swept into the motel room, slatted by the blinds. He switched on the free television and watched mindlessly for a few minutes; turned it off and went outside. The night's residual heat oozed out of the walls and pavements. The boulevards were all neon and incandescence, the lights of cars slid by, the snores of big trucks shook the air. Against the dusty sky the mountains were a vague heavier mass.

He walked across the motel apron to the sidewalk and went along the neon-lighted strip to a stucco building that sat by itself in a dusty gravel yard, *Schlitz* and *Coors* signs filling its windows; he went inside and got his bearings. It was a cheap saloon – eight wooden booths, dark scratched bar with cracked-upholstery

121

stools, glass-framed licenses, dusty snapshots, and half a dozen broken old guns on the wall.

There was a scatter of people in the place, hunched painfully over drinks, listening to the thump and whine of hillbilly records on the juke box. Several people looked at him, saw he wasn't an acquaintance and went back into themselves. Suddenly he didn't want this; he almost turned and left, but the bartender was giving him a big smile and a "Howdy there," and Paul went to an empty six-foot space at the bar and asked for a dry martini.

If his appearance hadn't identified him the martini order did; several sets of eyes flickered at him again. He took the drink across to an empty booth and sat down with his eyes half-closed and let the twanging music get into him. He didn't want to think; thinking had become painful.

Cowboy boots went thudding past; he looked up at the receding shape of a big man in a business suit and a white ten-gallon hat. He had an urge to snicker. The man in boots and hat left the place and Paul swept his glance along the bar, the people at the bar. They were all so anxious that strangers should like their desert city. The forced hospitality, the desperate boosterism. It was an alien country to him; he'd felt less out-of-place in Europe. *Sam Kreutzer would feel right at home, but not me.*

> *I hear that lonesome train*
> *Whistle down the rails;*
> *Sometimes I hear you call my name*
> *Down that far backtrail*
> *From Yuma, all the way from Yuma.*

The guitar and the fiddle and the rhythm, the woeful plains-twanging voice. Always sad songs about lost loves. No Gershwin and Porter and Rodgers out here; it was a foreign tongue.

He bought another drink and sat listening to the sad simple tunes. They made the past a troubled reality; he drank quickly and bought a third, and sat twirling the glass in his fingers. Remembering the times when everything existed in its ordered place, when you could tell right from wrong. Days of black telephones, two-decker buses on Park Avenue, ticker-tape parades for heroes you didn't laugh at, a pad of check blanks at every cash register, Grable and Gable and Hayworth and Cooper, an amiable cop on the beat, a fish wrapped in newspaper, clandestine dreams in plain brown wrappers, Uncle Irwin in the Depression wearing white shirts to prove to the world he could afford the laundry bill, the importance of chastity and the evils of alcohol and the goodness of Our American Boys, Pat O'Brien and apple pies and motherhood and tell-it-to-the-Marines and the *Darktown Strutters' Ball* and Glenn Miller's *Stardust. Jesus I remember Glen Miller. By crap yes I remember Glen Miller — very important to remember Glenn Miller.*

"My name's Shirley Mackenzie."

She was standing by his table with a glass in her hand, pushing the ice cubes around with a swizzle stick. He was so startled he only stared up at her. She wore a maroon velvet band across her dark hair. A narrow large-eyed face with succulent cushion lips. A thin body clad in a silvery blouse and a short leather skirt. She smiled a little, not brazenly. "You sort of look the way I feel. That's why I came over. I'll shove off if you want."

123

"No – no, don't. Sit down." He got clumsily out of the booth, remembering his manners.

"I don't really mean to intrude. I mean –"

"No, I could use some company."

"Only if you're sure." She had a good voice, low, half a whisky baritone. A walnut-brown face; when she turned into the light he saw she as a good deal older than he had thought at first. Thirty-five or so. Her nails were chewed down to the quick.

Standing there while she slid into the booth he realised he was perilously close to being very drunk: his vision was blurred, his balance uncertain, his tongue thick and clumsy. He got back into his seat and watched her across the table. "Paul. Paul Benjamin."

She acknowledged it with a vague smiling nod. "I don't suppose names really matter, do they. I mean ships that pass in the night and all that." Her lips quivered before she drew them in between her teeth. She had both hands wrapped around her drink.

"Well, then, Shirley Mackenzie."

"You remembered it. Think of that." Her face tipped to one side; the smile was wider now but filled with self-mockery.

"What did you mean, I look the way you feel?"

"Oh, sort of like the world had just fallen down around your ankles." She tossed her head back and lifted her glass, a faint gesture of toasting; ice clinked against her teeth and she put it down empty of everything but ice cubes. "Look I'm not a B-girl with a sob story if that's what you were thinking."

"At this point I'm not sure I'd mind."

"That's painfully honest. Honest for you, painful for me." She smiled yet again to show she wasn't offended.

"Would you like another?" He indicated her glass.

"Sure. I'll pay for it though." She lifted her shoulder-strap bag onto the table.

"Not necessary," he muttered awkwardly. "What was it?"

"Scotch and soda."

"Any brand?"

"Bar Scotch. I never could tell the difference."

He bought the two drinks and brought them back to the table. She didn't make a fuss about his having paid, but her bag was still on the table. He took a swallow and knew his mouth would taste rancid by midnight. *What the hell.* "So" he said, and stopped, unable to think of what to say.

"I'm sorry, I'm not much help either, am I. I'm not used to picking up strangers in bars."

"Neither am I."

They both smiled. Then the shape of her eyes changed. "Hate is a very exciting feeling, do you know that?"

"What do you mean?"

"I don't know, I was sitting over there at the bar thinking about killing my son of a bitch of a husband – ex-husband, pardon me. I mean really thinking about killing him. Imagining what it would be like to strangle him with piano wire or stick a kitchen knife in his throat. I'd never do it of course, I'm not that crazy. But do you ever have daydreams like that?"

"I guess so."

"It's exciting, isn't it? Gets all the juices flowing. You get very stimulated."

"You know that's true. . . ."

"You said that as if it's happened to you but you never recognized it before."

"Something like that, yes."

125

She shook her head – the same mockery again. "I guess you don't want to talk about yours either."

"My what?"

"Whatever it is that made the world fall down around your ankles. All right, we'll make a deal – we won't talk about any of that, we'll talk about something else. You live here?"

He widened his eyes. "Here? Tucson?"

"I guess you don't."

"I'm surprised – I thought it stuck out all over me. I'm from New York."

"Well if I were a local I'd probably have noticed. I'm from Los Angeles."

"On your way to or from?"

"From. Emphatically from. I got this far today – I'm staying in the motel next door."

"So am I."

It caused a brief gap; she dropped her eyes to her drink. Paul said, "Look, I didn't mean anything by that It wasn't a hint. I happen to be staying there, that's all."

"I am beginning to feel," she said in an abrupt vicious little voice, "like the world's prime cockteaser. Please forgive me."

"What for?"

"For coming on like some kind of nympho bar girl and then flying into a twitter the minute I imagine I hear you tossing a gentle pitch my way. I *am* sorry."

"Nothing to apologize for, I promise you." Another swallow: *Take it easy on this stuff.* "Where are you bound for, then?"

"Ask me tomorrow when I get in my car. Maybe I'll have an idea by then."

"You really are footloose and fancy-free."

A twisted smile, a dip of her face; her hair swung for-

126

ward, half masking her. "I have a sister in Houston. I suppose I'm edging in that direction. Reluctantly."

"No other family? No children?"

"Three kids." She bit it off. "My husband got them."

"I'm sorry. I didn't mean to pry."

"It's all right. All you'd have to do would be read the Los Angeles papers. It's public knowledge. I'm not fit to raise my own children – the judge said so."

"I'm sorry. Really."

"Of course it helps when your husband's a lawyer and the judge is a friend of his." Her face whipped up. "Do I look as if I'd neglect my chidren? . . . Shit, never mind, how could you be expected to answer that? Look, I promised we'd talk about something else. What are you doing here? Vacation?"

"Business. Very dull I'm afraid."

"All the way from New York. It must be big."

"Big for some people. For me it's just my job."

"What do you do? Or is that prying?"

"No, not at all. I'm a C.P.A., I'm doing an audit of a company's books. It's hardly a sensitive subject but I promise you it's less interesting than dishwater."

"Well, then. What shall we talk about? Nuclear submarines? The weather?"

"I don't mind, really."

"We don't really have to talk at all. It's such a strain sometimes, isn't it?" She gathered her handbag and tossed off the rest of the Scotch. "Why don't we go?" The voice was pert but she wasn't meeting his eyes.

He walked her across the motel's concrete apron, concentrating on his balance. She trailed along beside him with her vague involuted smile, her hips swaying from the slender stem of her waist. "The station wagon with mud all over it, that's me. My room."

127

"I'll say goodnight then, and good luck to you."

"No." She turned under the porch overhang. "Do you like me? Do you like me at all?"

"Yes – I do."

She opened the door; it hadn't been locked. She drew him inside and pushed the door shut behind him. The only light was what slotted in through the half-closed blinds. Against it her eyes glittered, betraying a wild desperate appetite. "I want to hold you. I want you to hold me. Please hold me for a minute. . . ."

He reached for her and they breathed liquor on each other, and kissed; he felt the tears on her cheeks. "Oh, come on to bed," she said, "we both seem to need it and it's a friendly thing for two people to do, isn't it? Isn't it?"

He awoke conscious of having dreamed. Weakness in all his fibres; a pounding dull headache, a dehydrated pain in his abdomen.

"You can open the other eye now, I've made some coffee."

He sat up and took the cup. His fingers were unsteady. He looked at her for the first time. She still had a red patch on her chin from his stubble.

The coffee made a good smell but it tasted terrible. He put the cup down half-full. "Thanks."

She was already dressed – the same blouse and leather skirt as last night. A good looking woman, he thought. Small, too thin, a little leathery around the eyes; but damned good looking. In the night he'd lain drowsily between sleeps, thinking what it would be like to live with a woman who could take his mind off the TV commercials and the killers in the alleys.

128

She said, "I'm all packed. I thought of letting you sleep it off, but it occurred to me it would be awkward if I left and the maid came in and found you here."

An abrupt tug in his throat; an instant's wistful panic. "You're going?"

"Time to hit the road. It's a long way to Houston." She patted her lips with a tissue, set the cup down in the saucer and stood in front of the mirror smoothing down her skirt. "Thank you for last night. I needed somebody to help me make it through to this morning."

It occurred to him as she went out the door that she probably didn't even remember his name.

"So long, Shirley Mackenzie."

He wasn't sure she heard him; the door continued to close. Clicked shut and left him very alone in the room.

"Oh, Jesus," he croaked, and began to cry.

It was Saturday; he spent the half day in the Jainchill conference room and had lunch at a franchise hamburger drive-in and drove toward the centre of town, down Speedway to Fourth Avenue and left down Fourth toward the tracks. The sporting goods store was where he remembered it. He went inside and said, "I'd like to buy a gun."

On the plane he dozed with his head against the plexiglas pane. The stewardess went down the aisle looking at passengers' seat belts; the lights of New York made a glow in the haze over the city. They circled down in the holding pattern and landed at Kennedy. In the terminal on his way to baggage-claim he stopped at a counter to pick up a present for Carol: she had always had a tooth for bitter chocolate. He bought half a dozen Dutch bars and put them in his briefcase on top of the papers which concealed the .32 calibre Smith & Wesson revolver and the six fifty-round boxes of ammunition.

He collected his suitcase and went out to the curb debating whether to spend the fifteen dollars on the taxi ride; in the end he took the airport limousine-bus to the East Side Terminal in Manhattan and a taxi home from there.

The apartment was stuffy although it was a cool night outside. He threw the windows open and took his briefcase into the bathroom where no one across the street could see inside; the pane was frosted. Lowered the lid of the toilet and sat down and took the revolver out, and held it in his fist staring at its black oily gleam.

14

He had it in his pocket when he went to work Thursday morning. He breathed shallowly in the jammed subway car but when someone caromed against him with a lurch of the car he shoved the offender away roughly: the gun was making him arrogant, he was going to have to watch that.

He rode the Shuttle across town in the same car with a Transit Patrolman who stood in the middle of the swaying car watching everybody with stony unimpressed eyes. Paul didn't meet them. He had spent ten minutes propping up mirrors in the apartment to look at himself from every angle and make sure the gun in his trouser pocket didn't make too obvious a bulge; he knew the cop had no way of detecting its presence but his nerves drew up to a twanging vibration and he hurried across the platform the instant the doors opened.

It was a very small gun, a compact five-shot model with a short barrel and a metal shroud over the hammer to prevent it from snagging on clothing. He had told the store clerk he wanted a little gun for his tackle-box, something that wouldn't crowd the reels and trout-flies and wouldn't get tangled in testlines. The clerk had tried to sell him a .22 single-shot pistol but Paul had declined it on the grounds that he wasn't a good enough shot to feel safe with only a single bullet. He had had to reject a .22 revolver as well and that had made the clerk smile knowingly and make an under-the-breath remark about how everybody ought to have the right to carry a gun in his glove-compartment and this ought to be just the thing don't you think?

It was mostly aluminium, very lightweight. Paul had asked if there was a target range in town where he might practice with the gun and the clerk had directed him to a rod-and-gun club ten miles up in the foothills; he had paid two dollars for the use of the range and had spent Saturday afternoon and all day Sunday burning up several hundred rounds of ammunition. By Sunday night his ears had been half-dead and ringing, and his right hand had been numb from the repeated recoil, but he was confident he could hit a man-size target from several yards' distance and for self-protection that was all you needed. Sunday night he had cleaned the gun meticulously and oiled it and wrapped it in a sock and fitted it carefully into the bottom of his briefcase. There had only been one bad moment – getting on the plane they had been searching the passengers; but he didn't look like a hijacker or a dope smuggler and he knew it. They looked down into the briefcase but didn't remove anything from it; he was passed through, politely enough, but he hadn't stopped sweating for an hour. After that he had filled up with outraged indignation against the twisted system of values that made it a criminal offence to carry the means of your own preservation. He was sure what he felt wasn't guilt; it was the fear of getting caught, which was a different thing. And they had no moral right to force a man to fear that sort of thing.

At any rate it was better than having to fear for your life. Only criminals and fools ever went to prison. If he were ever caught with the gun in his pocket it would be troublesome but he knew it wouldn't be critical; he had Jack, he knew several high-powered attorneys, and he had sufficient moral justification to insure that the worst

132

that could possibly happen would be a token conviction on some minor charge, a suspended sentence or a reprimand. The only ones who got jailed were the ones caught red-handed committing violent felonies, and even then if you had any brains you could find ways to avoid imprisonment. That was the trouble with the system. Last year Jack had defended a fifteen-year-old boy in Family Court accused of threatening a store-cashier with a knife and taking eighteen dollars from the till. The store had large signs everywhere announcing that the place was guarded by cameras but the fifteen-year-old boy couldn't read. They had picked him up within twenty-four hours. He was convicted not because of his crime but because of his illiteracy. "I had him cop a plea, of course," Jack had said wearily. "I hate making deals with prosecutors but that's the way things work. But do you know what the real frustration is? They'll teach that kid how to read but they won't teach him the difference between right and wrong. The odds are, a week after he gets out they'll nail him again for holding up a store that didn't have protective devices. Or he'll walk into a hockshop and try to rob the till and the storekeeper will blow his head off."

At the time it had seemed sad. Now Paul was thoroughly on the side of the storekeeper.

Jack, he thought. When the welcome-backs and the hearty shouts were dispensed with he went to the desk and phoned Jack's office. "I tried to get you earlier."

"I was at the hospital."

His fingers reached the desk and gripped its edge. "You sound terrible. What is it?"

"Not now – not through two switchboards. Look Pop, can we meet somewhere – around lunchtime? I've juggled my calendar, I've got two court cases this morning but I'll be free after eleven-thirty or so if things don't back up in court."

"Of course. But can't you at least –"

"I'd rather not. Look, suppose I come up to your office. I ought to get there about noon. Wait for me, will you?"

He spent most of the morning in the computer room feeding figures to the programmers. It was easier than thinking. Jack had never been the kind who hinted at mysteries; he wasn't playing a game. It had to be something to do with Carol – but that was all the more puzzling. Paul had phoned last night, he had kept in constant touch from Arizona, and nothing had occurred that hadn't been predicted – Carol was responding to therapy, the doctors expected to release her within a few weeks. . . .

He was back in his office by ten minutes to twelve. When Thelma buzzed he pounced on the intercom but she said, "It's Mr. Kreutzer."

Sam came loping through the door with a slothful smile beneath his moustache. "Well, how was it out there in all that sunshine?"

"Fine – fine."

"How about lunch? Bill and I thought we'd just pop downstairs and grab a liverwurst. Join us?"

"Afraid I can't. Jack's coming by any minute."

"We'll squeeze him in, what the hell. We don't discriminate against lawyers."

"No, it's family business. I'll take a raincheck. How's Adele?"

"Just fine. Kind of worried about you. She seems to feel we owe you an apology for that night. You were pretty upset, understandably, and I guess we shouldn't have jumped all over you that way. Forgiven?"

"Sure, Sam. Nothing to forgive."

"Then you won't turn down an invitation. It's our fifteenth, two weeks from tomorrow – that's Friday the third. We're having a little anniversary get-together at our place. No presents, we're adamant about that. Just bring yourself. Right?"

"Well – yes. Thanks, Sam. I'll be there."

"Great, great. Write it down in your calendar so you won't forget it." Sam glanced at his watch and shot his cuff. "Well, I'll toddle along. See you." And went.

By twelve-fifteen Paul had started to fidget. He drew a heavily crosshatched doodle around the Kreutzers' party in his appointment book; went down the hall and washed his hands; came back to the office expecting to find Jack waiting, and found it empty and sat behind the desk fooling with the revolver.

When the intercom buzzed he shoved the gun quickly into his pocket and looked up as the door opened and Jack came in dragging his heels, his eyes faded and his drooping pinched mouth suggesting dejection and anxiety. He kicked the door shut behind him.

"Well, what is it?"

"Let me sit down." Jack went to the leather chair and sank into it like a fighter collapsing on a ring-corner stool after the fifteenth round. "Christ, it's hot for this time of year."

"What's the matter with Carol, Jack?"

"Everything."

"But she was getting on so well –"

"Not all that well, Pop. I didn't see any point getting you all disturbed over it on long-distance telephones. I put a better face on it than the facts deserved."

135

"I see."

"Please don't do the chilly number on me, Pop. I thought it was best at the time. What was the point of worrying you? You'd only have loused up your work, or quit altogether and flown back here. There wasn't a thing you could do. They haven't even let *me* see her in two weeks."

"Then I would suggest," Paul said through his teeth, "that we hire ourselves another psychiatrist. This man sounds as if he belongs in an institution himself."

Jack shook his head. "No, he's all right. We've had consultations with three other shrinks. They're all pretty much agreed. One of them voted against the insulin therapy but other than that they've all subscribed to the same diagnosis and the same program of treatment. It isn't their fault, Pop. It just hasn't worked."

"What are you telling me?"

"Pop, they've tried hypnosis, they've tried insulin shock twice, and it just hasn't worked. She's not responding. She keeps drawing farther back into that shell every day. Do you want the technical jargon? I can reel out yards of it and cut it to fit, I've been listening to it for weeks. Catatonia. Dementia praecox. Passive schizoid paranoia. They've been slinging Freudian argot around like bricks. It boils down to the fact that she had an experience she couldn't face and she's running away from it, inside herself."

Jack covered his face with his hands. "God, Pop, she's nothing but a God-damned vegetable now."

He sat blinking across the desk at the top of Jack's lowered head. He knew the question he had to ask; he had to force himself to ask it. "What do they want to do, then?"

Jack's answer was a long time coming. Finally he lif-

136

ted his face. His cheeks were gray; his eyes had gone opaque. "They want me to sign papers to commit her."

It hit him in waves. His scalp shrank.

Jack said, "It's my decision and I'll make it, but I want your advice."

"Is there an alternative?"

Jack spread his hands wide and waved them helplessly.

"What happens if you don't sign the papers?"

"Nothing, I suppose. They'll keep her in the hospital. The insurance is about to run out. When we run out of money the hospital will throw her out." Jack's head was swinging back and forth rhythmically – worn-out, dazed. "Pop, she can't even *feed* herself."

"And if she's committed? What then?"

"I've checked. I have a policy that covers it, up to six hundred a month. Doctor Metz recommended a sanitarium out in New Jersey. They charge a little more than that but I can swing the difference. It's not the money, Pop."

"This commitment – is it a one-way thing?"

"Nobody can answer that. Sometimes after a few months of therapy they come out of it themselves. Sometimes they never do."

"Then what are you asking me?"

He watched anguish change Jack's features. "Look, I love her."

". . . . Yes," very gentle.

"You don't just throw somebody you love into an institution and turn your back. You just can't."

"No one seems to be asking us to turn our backs."

"I could take her home," Jack muttered. "I could feed her and wash her and carry her into the bathroom."

137

"And how long could you last doing that?"

"I could hire a private nurse."

"You still couldn't live that way, Jack."

"I know. Rosen and Metz keep saying the same thing."

"Then we've got no alternative, really. Have we."

When Jack left he took the gun out of his pocket. It was what had kept him from going to pieces. The refrain in his mind: the killers. *So. Now they add this to their debts.*

They've got no right to do this to us. To anybody. They've got to be stopped.

15

He took the Lexington Avenue line uptown to Sixty-eighth. Had dinner in a counter place, walked by dogleg blocks to Seventy-second and Fifth, and went into Central Park there, walking crosstown. It wasn't fully dark yet – dusk, and a cool grey wind, leaves falling, people walking their dogs. The street lamps were lit but it was a poor light for vision.

He walked slowly as if exhausted by a long day's hard work. This was the time of night when they came out from under their rocks to prey on tired home-bound pedestrians. *All right*, he thought, *prey on me*.

The anger in him was beyond containment. It was a chilly night and he wasn't the only solitary pedestrian in the park with his hands rammed into his pockets. He didn't look like an armed man. *Come on. Come and get it.*

Two youths: Levi's, scraggy hair down to their shoulders, acned faces. Coming toward him with their thumbs hooked in their belts. Looking for trouble. *Come get some, then.*

They went right past without even glancing at him; he caught a waft of conversation: "... a bummer, man, a real down. Worst fucking movie ever made. ..."

Two kids on their way home from a movie. Well they shouldn't dress like hoodlums; it was asking for trouble.

The twilight had gone completely, behind the high monoliths of Central Park West; the light was failing quickly. He walked along the path with a light traffic of theater-bound taxis sliding through the crosstown loop beside him. A blatant homosexual with two huge hairy dogs on leashes went past him with an arch petulant expression. Two elderly couples strolling, guarded by a leashed Doberman. Three young couples, smartly dressed, hurrying past him, obviously late for a curtain at Lincoln Center.

A cop on a scooter, his white helmet turning to indicate his interest in Paul: every solitary pedestrian was suspect. Paul gave the cop a straight look. The scooter buzzed away.

He stopped midway across the park and sat down on a bench and watched people walk by until it got to be wholly night-dark. In his pocket, sweat lubricated the handle of the gun in his fist. He got up and continued his walk.

Central Park West. He turned north a block and cut across on Seventy-third because you weren't too likely to get mugged on Seventy-second, it was too crowded. Columbus Avenue. Now the dark long block to the Amsterdam-Broadway triangle.

Nothing. He crossed the square and glanced up Broadway. That was the bar where he'd listened to the beer-drinker complain about welfare-niggers. Seventy-fourth, a block from here – that was where the kid with the knife had come at him from behind. *Try it again now.*

Carol. . . . It was too much to bear.

Seventy-third and West End Avenue. He stood under the street light looking downtown toward his apartment building two blocks south. Nothing sinister between here and there. *Damn. Where the hell are you?*

Getting chilly.

But he turned uptown instead. Went up to Seventy-fourth and crossed back to Amsterdam Avenue. Midway along the block – he even recognized the flight of stone stairs where he'd half-collapsed after the kid had run away. He had the block to himself again tonight but no one came at him.

Amsterdam: he walked around the corner and uptown with longer strides. Up into the West Eighties. Mixed neighborhoods now, stately co-ops shouldering against tenements. He had never walked here at night before. The sense of urban ferment was too strong: dark kids on front steps, old people at windows.

Feet getting tired now. Colder too. He reached an intersection and checked the sign: Eighty-ninth and Columbus. He turned west.

Two youths on the kerb – Puerto Ricans in thin wind-breakers. *Okay, come on.* But they only watched him go past. *Do I look too tough? What's the matter with you, don't I look like an easy mark? You only pick on women?*

Now that's unfair. Get hold of yourself. They're probably as honest as you are.

Riverside Drive. A party was going on in one of the apartments overhead: the wind blew gusts of rock music to him; a paper cup came fluttering down from the open window – the excretum of civilized pleasures. Half a block farther down, three young men were loading suitcases into a Volkswagen – the standard stagger system: one carrying bags out, another going in for another load, the third guarding the car. *It's insane. No one should have to.* He crossed the Drive and went along to the stairs.

Down into Riverside Park.

The trees were flimsy against the lights. Traffic rushed

along the Henry Hudson. He moved through the paths, past the playground, along the slopes. A copse of ragged smog-stunted trees; here the darkness had the viscosity of syrup and he suddenly felt an atavistic twinge: *You're in here, I can feel you. Watching me, waiting for me. Come on then.* But he penetrated the trees and no one was there. On along the path: the end of the park up ahead, the steps up to the Drive, Seventy-second Street not far beyond. He thought with savage sarcasm, *All right it's a poor night for hunting. But you'll come after me again, won't you.*

He was cold clear through; his feet were sore. He went straight for the steps. It was only a few blocks to the apartment.

Approaching the steps he caught a tail-of-the-eye movement imperfectly and then the soft insinuating voice:

"Hey, wait a minute."

Paul stopped. Turned.

A tall man, very tall. Thin to the point of emaciation, stooped. Clad in a thin jacket too short at the wrists. A hollow death's-head, shoulders that twitched nervously. The hair was either pale red or blond. The knife was a fixed-blade hunting-knife, wicked in the dimness. "You got any money on you, buddy?"

"I might."

"Hand – hand it over." The knife came up two inches; the empty left hand beckoned. The junkie licked his upper lip like a cat washing itself, and ventured toward Paul.

"This is it, then," he breathed.

"What? Hey, gimme the money, man."

"You're going to get in a lot of trouble."

A quick pace forward. The junkie loomed, hardly be-

yond arm's length. "Hey I don't want to cut you. Now
hand it over and beat it, huh?" The voice was a nervous
whine but maybe that was the dope in him, or the lack
of it; the knife was steady enough, blade-up, the fist
locked around it in a way that showed he knew how to
use it.

Don't talk to him. Just do it.

"Man the *money*!"

He took it out of his pocket and pulled the trigger
three times and the junkie stumbled back: his hands
clutched the wounds, trying to hold the blood in, and
the skull-face took on an expression of pained indignation rather than anger. He caromed off the iron railing
and fell on his side without using his arms to break his
fall. Paul was ready to fire again but the junkie didn't
move.

Drunk with it he stumbled into the apartment and
stood sweating, quivering in every rigid limb, needles in
his legs; soaked in his own juices.

"Uh-huh," he said. "Uh-huh, uh-huh."

16

There was no mention in the *Times*. The *Daily News* had two brief paragraphs on page ten: *PAROLEE SLAIN IN R'SIDE PARK*. "Thomas Leroy Marston, 24, was found shot to death last night in Riverside Park. Marston had been released from Attica State Penitentiary two weeks ago on parole after serving forty-two months of a five-year sentence for grand larceny.

"At his sentencing three years ago Marston admitted he had been a heroin addict. Police refused to guess whether his death was connected with drugs. Marston was shot three times by a small-calibre revolver. The assailant, or assailants, have not been apprehended."

The police were looking for him. It was only to be expected. They weren't likely to find him. It was easy to read between the lines in the *News*. The police were theorizing that Marston had tried to double-cross a dope pusher and the pusher had shot him. Fine; let them drag some of the pushers off the streets for questioning.

But he was going to have to be more careful in the future. He had made several mistakes; half the night he had sat in the living-room with the gun on the table in front of him, coolly assessing the events. There were several mistakes, mainly of omission. He had not stopped to make sure Marston was dead. He had not disguised himself in any way; if there had been an eyewitness he would have been too easily identified. He had come straight home and it was possible the doorman, if ever questioned, might remember the time of Paul's arrival.

In the future. *What is it that I'm planning to do?*

To hell with it. He wasn't going to lie to himself. The streets and parks were public places. He had a right to use them whenever he chose. And anyone who tried to attack him or rob him would have to take his chances.

Friday evening he met Jack at a Steak & Brew and they talked about the technicalities of the commitment. Paul contained his grief by channeling it to anger; he was resigned to Carol's pain and his own loss; beginning to think less of his own agonies and more of those who hadn't been victimized yet. By stopping Marston he had prevented God knew how many future crimes from happening.

He took a cab straight home and stared at the television until he fell asleep in front of the set.

Saturday he awoke with a throbbing headache. He'd had nothing to drink the night before; he couldn't understand it. Possibly the air pollution. He swallowed aspirins and went across the street to the Shopwell to get groceries for the week. He had to stand in a slow line at the check-out counter; the headache was maddening and he wanted to elbow his way straight to the cash register. The headache dissipated during the morning but by midafternoon it had returned; he tossed the crossword puzzle on the floor and decided to take a nap, sleep it off.

It was dark when he came to. The darkness unnerved him; he went around the place switching on lights. When he looked at his watch he found it was nearly nine o'clock. *Christ I can't spend another night in this place. Maybe a movie.* He examined the newspaper listings; the only thing worth trying was the double-bill rerun of James Bond films – he didn't have the patience for an

145

intellectual artsy picture and everything else was porno-graphic dreck.

The features ran at even-numbered hours but it didn't matter. He took the subway local to Fiftieth Street and walked down Broadway to the theater. Entered the auditorium in the midst of a Technicolor car-chase and found his way to a seat and let the choreographed wide-screen violence absorb him.

The second film ended with someone being crushed to death in an enormous machine that reduced an auto-mobile to a chair-sized cube of metal. He left the theater shortly before midnight, too restless to sit through the first half of the other film.

After the spectacular sound-volume of the theater's speakers the racket of Times Square seemed muted and unreal. He stopped to get his bearings, feeling strange and oddly guilty: he had never gone to movies by him-self and he felt as if someone had just caught him mas-turbating. Once a long time ago he had been briefly in San Francisco over a week-end, waiting for his Army dis-charge; he had spent most of Saturday and all day Sun-day going from one triple-feature to another. He had seen eleven movies – seven of them Westerns – in those two days. It was the nearest thing to a Lost Weekend he had ever experienced. After six months behind a type-writer in Okinawa and nearly two seasick weeks on a troopship he had owned no strength to take in the sights of San Francisco or enjoy its notorious night pleasures; he had lost himself in the never-never land of Tex Ritter and John Wayne and Richard Dix and Bela Lugosi.

Times Square was a running sore, jostling with the chalky bodies of hookers, open-mouthed tourists, swag-gering male prostitutes, men slipping furtively into peep-show theaters and porno bookstores. Cops in pairs every

146

few yards: they were all on the take because if they weren't, half the people in sight would be under arrest. These were the dregs, this was their cesspool. Their dreary faces slid by in the overpowering neon daylight and Paul turned quickly uptown, full of angry disgust.

Out of the tinsel, up toward Fifty-seventh. The new car showrooms, the groups in good clothes on the corners looking for taxis to take them home from their after-theater dinners.

A cop on the corner, the steady watchfulness of his eyes: Paul walked past and felt his face twitch. Before he had done it, he had been convinced there was no danger: they could never get him. But now it had happened and he was beginning to think of a hundred ways they could find him. A witness? Fingerprints – had he touched anything? He felt his face flaming; he went on into Columbus Circle, clutching the gun in his pocket. Suppose a cop stopped him and asked him something: could he handle it? He was such a poor dissembler.

The Coliseum, now the handsome buildings of Lincoln Center looking like something miraculously spared by the bombing attacks that had reduced the surrounding neighborhood to gray rubble. The city had the look and feel of occupation: the walk up Broadway was a combat mission behind enemy lines and you never met the eyes of the hurrying head-down strangers you passed.

That was it, then, he thought; he was the first of the Resistance – the first soldier of the underground.

Monday in the lunch hour he went down into the Village and browsed the shops on Eighth Street and Greenwich Avenue and then on Fourteenth Street. At different shops he bought a dark roll-neck sweater, a re-

147

versible jacket with dark gray on one side and bright hunter's red on the other, a cabbie's soft cap, a pair of lemon-colored gloves.

Before ten that evening he took a bus up to Ninety-sixth Street and walked across town into Central Park. The tennis courts and the reservoir were to the right; he crossed the transverse to the left and walked along above the ball-playing fields. He was wearing the cap and the jacket gray-side-out. *Come on, now.*

But he walked all the way through the Park without seeing anyone except two bicyclists.

Well everyone was afraid of the Park nowadays. The muggers knew that; they had shifted their hunting grounds elsewhere. He nodded at the discovery – now he knew; he wouldn't make this mistake again.

At the Fifth Avenue wall he made a turn around the children's playground and started to walk back up toward the transverse but then in a chip of light between the trees he saw a motionless figure on a park bench and something triggered all his warning systems: the short hairs prickled at the back of his neck and he moved forward slowly through the trees, letting his breath trickle out slowly through his mouth. Something was stirring there – he had picked up movement, as insubstantial as fog, but it was there. He stopped, watched. He had to fight a cough down.

It was an old man slumped on the bench; probably a drunk. Wrapped in a ragged old coat, huddling it to him. That wasn't what had alerted Paul; there was someone else.

Then he spotted the shadow. Slipping slowly along behind the park bench, moving up from the drunk's blind side.

Paul waited. It might be a curious kid, harmless; it might even be a cop. But he didn't think so. The stealthy purpose, the careful stalking silence.... Into the light now: a man in skin-tight trousers and a leather jacket and an Anzac hat cocked over one eye. Moving without sound to the back of the bench and looking down at the sleeping drunk.

The intruder's head lifted and turned: he scanned his horizons slowly and Paul stood frozen, not breathing. Fingers curling around the gun in his pocket.

The black man came around the end of the park bench and as he stepped onto the path his hand came out in sight and Paul heard the crisp snap as the knife flicked open. *He's going to rob that poor drunk.*

The black man looked around again before he turned and crouched down by the drunk. Paul stepped forward through the trees. "Stand up," very soft.

From his crouch the intruder broke into an immediate run. Racing toward the safety of the farther trees.

Paul fired.

The gunshot arrested the black man: he stopped and wheeled.

He thinks I'm a cop.

Well, that wasn't a miss, you son of a bitch. It was just to turn you around so you can watch me shoot you. He trembled in rage: he lifted the revolver and stared into the black man's eyes, hard as glass. The man was lifting his hands into the air in surrender. The sight of his vicious sneering face electrified the skin of Paul's spine.

He stepped forward into the light because it was important that the intruder see him. A muscle worked at the back of the black man's jaw. Then the face changed: "Hey, man, what's goin' down?"

Flame streaked out of Paul's gunbarrel; the shot laid hard echoes across the blacktop path and the firecracker stink of the smoke got into his nostrils.

The bullet plunged into the abdomen, rupturing it with a subcutaneous explosion of gases. Paul fired again; the black man fell back, turned, began to scramble toward the trees.

It was remarkable how much a human body could take and still keep functioning. He fired twice more into the back of the man's head. It dropped him.

Paul glanced at the drunk. The drunk hadn't even stirred. He was facing the other way, half-lying on the bench. Was he alive at all?

Paul crossed to the black man and looked at him. There were flecks of white saliva at the corners of the man's mouth. His face was twisted to the side and the eyes stared blankly at nothing. His sphincter muscles had failed and an unmistakable odour hung around the body in a cloud.

Paul hurried to the drunk. The man was snoring softly.

He faded back into the trees along the bridle path. There might be a cop nearby. He hurried up toward the fence that surrounded the reservoir; just before he reached it he turned to the right and went along the side of the steep wooded slope, parallel to the fence but below it so that no one would see him silhouetted. Every few seconds he stopped and listened.

People would have heard the noise of the shots but no one would have a fix on it and they'd rationalize it had been a backfiring truck. It wouldn't be reported. Gunshots never were. The only real risk was that someone might have seen something. A passing pedestrian he hadn't spotted, or even another drunk lying concealed in the wood. He slipped out of the jacket and reversed it to show the bright red side; put the cap in his pocket and the gloves with it. The gun was back in his right front trouser pocket – the gun together with a rubber-banded roll of four hundred dollars in twenty dollar bills. If a cop decided for some reason to stop him and search him, Paul wanted the cop to find the four hundred dollars. It might work; he understood such things worked.

He went along the slope, losing his footing here and there on the slippery grass; he cut between the reservoir and the tennis courts and made his way across the oval drive and out of the Park by the Ninety-sixth Street gate. He felt exposed and vulnerable; he was sweating lightly in the cool air. Rickety and weak: but it was *real*, the lusting angry violence most people had never remotely tasted and would never understand. . . .

In his mailbox he found a folded mimeographed flyer letterheaded with the legend of the West End Avenue Block Association and signed in the facsimile handwriting of Herbert Epstein.

Dear West End Avenue Resident:
   The residents of this neighbourhood are understandably and gravely concerned with the priority-matter of SAFETY on the streets.
   Police statistics show that addicts and muggers are most likely to prey on the citizenry on dark, or poorly illuminated, streets; and that improved lighting on city streets has been demonstrated to cut crime as much as 75 percent.
   Your Block Association hopes to purchase and install a system of total-saturation street lighting

along West End Avenue and the side streets from 70th to 74th.

City funds are not available for this type of installation. Many neighborhood associations have already exercised initiative in purchasing high-saturation lighting in their areas. The cost per light is $350; within the area of our Block Association, individual contributions of as little as $7 each will enable us to saturate our neighborhood with bright lights and drive the criminals away into darker areas.

Your contribution is tax deductable. Please contribute as much as you can, for your own safety.

With sincere thanks,

Herbert Epstein

He left it open on his desk so he would remember to make out a check.

Years ago he had spent some of his weekends visiting his uncle and aunt in Rockaway. You could tell the rank and importance of the local mobsters by the brightness of the floodlights around their houses: they were the only people who had reason to fear for their lives.

Tuesday they took Carol to the rest home near Princeton. It was the first time he had seen her in weeks and although he had prepared himself he couldn't help showing his shock. She looked twenty years older. There was no trace of the coltish girl with the sweet and touching smile. She might as well have been a display-window mannequin.

Jack kept talking to her in his gentle voice – cheerful meaningless talk, the kind you would use to soothe a skittish horse – but there was no sign she heard any of it; there was no sign she was aware of her own existence, let alone anyone else's. *They have this to pay for,* he thought.

On the Amtrak train back to the city he sat beside Jack looking out the window at the slanting gray rain. Jack didn't speak. He seemed worn out by the fruitless effort to reach Carol. Paul tried to think of something comforting to say but he quickly realized there was nothing.

There was a peculiar gratification in seeing how badly Jack was taking it. It made Paul feel the stronger of the two. He wasn't breaking down at all; he was taking it in his stride.

But then his thoughts turned inward and he saw there was no reason to be smug; he was keeping his own equilibrium only because he seemed to have been struck by the edge of the same malaise that had infected Carol – the inability to feel anything. It was as if a transparent shield had been erected around him – as if his emotional center had been anesthetized. It had been closing in around him for several days, he realized. He remembered the mugger in Riverside Park: that had terrified him; but it was the last time he had known real fear. The second time – the man who'd tried to rob the drunk – he'd felt very little; he remembered it with vague detachment as if it were a scene from a movie he'd watched a long time ago.

He walked the streets that night but no one attacked him. At midnight he went home.

17

Wednesday morning from the office he telephoned Lieutenant Briggs, the Homicide detective. The police had nothing to report by way of progress in apprehending the intruders who had killed Esther and destroyed Carol's life. Paul summoned enough righteous outrage to reduce the lieutenant to a string of whining apologies and excuses.

When he hung up he realized how counterfeit his indignant outburst had been. He had done it on impulse because it seemed to be the thing that was expected of him and he didn't want to attract suspicion by any hint of unusual behavior. He was finding it surprisingly easy to act the innocent role: easy to be the injured helpless citizen, easy to look straight into people's faces without fear that his guilt would show. How quickly he had picked up the habit of guarding his secrets – as if he had been allowed to write out his own letters of reference, leaving out everything except what he chose to put in.

That night he decided to invade a new part of the wilderness. He took the subway down to Fourteenth Street and walked over into the truck district underneath the West Side Highway. Drunks slept beneath the overhanging loading platforms of the warehouses; the huge gray doors to the loading bays were locked formidably. On the side streets under the shadow of the elevated highway the light was very poor and the big trucks were lined up in uneven rows, half blocking the narrow passages. The air was cold and heavy; it wasn't raining but it had the feel of rain. The still thick night seemed to blot up light.

He found a car parked askew to the curb, as if it had been disabled and its driver had pushed it out of the center of the roadway and gone for help. The car had been stripped: the hood was up, the trunk-lid up, the car propped on bricks and stones. Its wheels and tyres were gone. He looked under the hood: the battery had been removed. The window of the driver's door had been smashed in. When he looked at the raised trunk-lid he saw it had been pried open; the lip of it was badly mangled. Six hours ago it might have been a good car with a leaf in the fuel line or an empty gas tank; now it was a gutted derelict.

A lump of hot rage grew in his belly.

Set a trap for them, he thought. There had to be a way. He kept walking, gripping the gun in his pocket, and after a little while he had it worked out in his mind.

Wednesday morning he phoned a rent-a-car office and reserved a car for overnight use.

At half-past ten he drove down the West Side Highway to the Eighteenth Street ramp and went rattling down the chuckholed exit to the warehouse district. On Sixteenth Street a police cruiser rolled slowly past him and the cops inside gave him an incurious glance. He went around the block and found a spot between two double-parked trucks on the right-hand side of the street, away from the street lights. He parked the car there at an awkward angle and wrote in a crabbed hand on a scrap of paper, "*Out of gas – back soon*," and stuck it under the windshield-wiper blade. It was the sort of

155

thing motorists did to avoid getting tickets. He locked the doors conscientiously and walked away from the car making a show of his disgust; went around the corner and quickly continued around the entire block; and posted himself in the shadows diagonally across the street from the car. He stood between the close-parked trailers of two semi-rig trucks, with a good field of view and good cover in the deep shadows.

Now and then a car went by. A pair of homosexual pedestrians, walking fast out of fear, touching each other intimately and laughing. He had heard the faggots sometimes drifted "the trucks" in search of pick-ups. It was the first time he'd seen it.

He found them vaguely revolting; they induced the same kind of discomfort he experienced when he had to look at a cripple. There was always something deeply disturbing about deformities you weren't used to and couldn't understand. But they were no threat to anyone except themselves and he had no impulse to do anything but let them go by. Fools, he thought, wandering this area at night unarmed. *They're asking for it.*

He backed up: that was wrong. They had a right to walk unmolested; everyone did.

Someone had to guard the city. Obviously the cops weren't doing it. He'd spent quite a bit of time in this neighbourhood two nights in a row and he'd only seen one passing patrol car.

Then it's up to me, isn't it?

He had to wait nearly an hour but finally they came – two thin boys in a battered old station wagon. They drove past the parked rental car at first. Went by it very slowly, the boy in the passenger seat rolling down his window and craning his neck out to read the little message under the wiper. Paul tensed. The two boys were in animated conversation but he couldn't hear their words; then the station wagon gunned away and he eased back between the two trailers. He would give it another half hour and then call it a night.

It came down the street again. The old station wagon. Rolled to a stop in front of Paul's car.

They'd gone around the block then. To make sure there weren't any cops.

They got out of the station wagon and opened its tailgate. He watched them remove tools – a crowbar, something else. Very professional.

When they opened the hood of his car Paul shot them both.

18

Thursday he returned the car to the agency before he went to work. He spent most of the day in the corner office with Henry Ives and George Eng going over the collated Jainchill figures. He had trouble keeping his mind on the subject at hand. George Eng was among the liberal wealthy; he lived behind the barricades of a great Park Avenue apartment house and sent his children to a private school but even so he spent twenty minutes that afternoon in bitter indignant complaint about the savage adolescents who extorted money from kids outside the school and, if they didn't have any, beat them up for sport. Eng's younger son had come home a few days ago bruised and limping. The police hadn't found his attackers. Eng's son wasn't reticent about it; it was just that they had been strangers to him. Public school kids, or dropouts; they were taking to hanging around private schools waiting for the students to come out.

He had dinner with Jack and they talked pointlessly about Carol. Jack had been out to see her yesterday; there was no change. Every day left room for a little less hope.

Later that night in the East Village he shot a man coming down a fire escape with a portable TV set.

It had been a slow weekend for news. Somewhere along the line the police had begun to make connections and the story made the Saturday evening newscasts and the front page of the Sunday *Times* as well as its editorial page.

A VIGILANTE IN THE STREETS?

Three men, all with criminal records, and two teen-age boys with narcotics arrest records, have been found shot to death in four Manhattan areas within the past ten days – all five shot by bullets from the same revolver, according to the police.

Deputy Inspector Frank Ochoa, placed in charge of the case on Friday, is calling it "the vigilante case." Inspector Ochoa said no connection has been found among the five victims except for their "criminal tendencies" and the fact that post-mortem ballistics tests have shown that all five were killed by bullets from the same .32 revolver.

From circumstantial evidence the police theorize that all five victims may have been engaged in criminal acts at the time of their deaths. Three of them, including the two 17-year-old boys (the only two of the five who were found dead at the same place and time), were found under suggestive circumstances. The two boys were found in the midst of a station wagon-load of car-stripping tools. The most recent victim, George Lambert, 22, was found with a stolen television set at the foot of a fire escape leading down from the window of an apartment from which the set had been stolen. The window showed signs of forcible entry.

The other two victims, found in upper Manhattan parks, may have been engaged in narcotics trading or armed robbery. Both were armed with knives.

These facts have led the police to the tentative conclusion that a self-styled one-man vigilante force is stalking the city with a .32 revolver. "It has to be some guy looking for retribution," Inspector Ochoa believes. "Some nut that thinks he's a one-man police force."

Inspector Ochoa has assigned a special detail to the case. "We're beginning to put it all together. Until a couple of days ago these cases were all in separate Precincts, which is why we've been a little slow making the connection. But we're on it now and the Department expects to apprehend the killer very quickly."

By the next morning the newspapers had picked it up with full energy. Inspector Ochoa was the *Times*'s Man-in-the-News. In the *Daily News* on the editorial page the *Inquiring Fotographer*'s man-in-the-street question was, "How do you feel about the vigilante killer?" and the six answers ranged from "You can't take the law into your own hands" to "They ought to leave that guy alone, he's doing what the cops should have done a long time ago." The afternoon *Post* editorialized, "Murder answers no questions. The vigilante must be nailed before he murders any more victims. We urge the Manhattan D.A. and the NYPD to spare no effort to bring the psychopath to justice."

He got up in the middle of the night. The sleeping pills weren't working very well any more. He made a cup of tea and re-read the newspaper accounts. The cup and saucer rattled in his hand, the tea rumbled uneasily in his stomach; he heard himself whimper softly.

There was no appeasement of his distress. He was

miserably lonely; he didn't want to spend the night with a woman – he didn't want to spend the night at all. He thought of Ochoa and his special detail: they were out there somewhere, ambitious men stalking *him* when they should have been guarding the honest citizens. An entire city slashing itself to extinction and all the police could do was search for the man who was trying to show them the way back.

It was a little after three. He didn't go back to bed. He had cleaned the gun since its last firing but he cleaned it again and sat a long time debating whether to continue carrying it in his pocket all the time. It might be safer to find a hiding place for it. As far as he knew, he had left no clues that would lead the police to him; but their technology was impressive and it was possible some hint might cause them to question him at some point. It would be better not to have the gun on him.

But there was no place to hide it. If they became suspicious of him they would surely search his apartment and his office. Other than those two places there was no other cache that would be safe and easily accessible. He thought up elaborate schemes worthy of gothic horror stories: digging out a brick in the basement, hiding the gun behind it – but all those were risky notions. A small boy might stumble on the hiding place; the building handyman might find it. The gun was the only positive and irrevocable connection between him and the killings. If the police ever got their hands on it they could match it up to the death bullets, and they could trace it to him effortlessly because the gun's serial number was registered to him in Washington through the dealer who'd sold it to him in Arizona.

Half-past four in the morning. His thoughts pendulumed from extreme to extreme. If they caught him he would kill himself, it was the clean neat way. No. If they caught him he would fight it out in the courts; he would get the best lawyers and they would have public sympathy on their side.

It wasn't inevitable that he would be caught. They had no objective cause to suspect him, as long as he was careful. His campaign was a reasoned one, not the result of mindless compulsions; he could pick and choose his time and place, he could suspend his operations until things cooled off. He had the options of free will. The editorialists were wrong of course; he wasn't psychotic, it wasn't an uncontrollable obsession, he wasn't compelled by diseased brain-cells to keep slaughtering innocent victims until he was caught – he was no crazy strangler begging for punishment through self-hate. *I'm a nut, of course*, he thought, but it was only by comparison with the insane norms of society that he was abnormal. What he was doing was extreme. But it was necessary. Someone had to do it: someone had to show the way.

"You can see it in the kids," George Eng said. "They used to be anti-police. Not any more. My kids are pro-cop with a vengeance. Can you blame them? The junkies are looting everything. Ripping off school calculators and lab equipment, mugging the kids. My son has a friend in one of the schools up in Westchester – they had to close the school this week. Vandals. They flooded the building with fire hoses – ransacked the place, urinated on the chairs, splashed paint all over the walls. I'll tell you something, this fellow who's out there killing them may be doing us all a service. Do you know we've got sixty-eight tenant families in my building and forty-one of them keep Dobermans and German shepherds? There

162

a seat by the door. An ancient wino slept on the opposite seat; two burly blacks with lunch pails sat at the end of the car.

The train crash-crashed through the Eighteenth Street local station without stopping. A Transit Patrolman walked through the car and stopped to shake the wino awake and give him a lecture; Paul couldn't hear the words. The cop got the wino on his feet and prodded him ahead through the door at the car-end vestibule. When it opened, sound rushed in, and a cold wind. The door slid part-way shut and lodged there. One of the black workmen got up and pushed it closed.

At Penn Station the workmen got off and Paul was alone in the car. The line's green traffic lights whipped past the filthy windows. He began to read the advertising placards above them.

The train screeched into the lights of the Times Square station and threw Paul around on the seat when it braked to a sharp halt. Two tough kids entered the car and sat down facing Paul. *Hubcap collectors*, he thought drily. They gave him insolent looks and one of them took out a pocket knife, opened it and began to clean his fingernails.

You could tell they were scum by looking at them. How many old women had they mugged? How many tenement shops had they knocked over?

The earsplitting racket of the train would cover the sound of the shots. He could leave them dead in the car and they might not be found until the train got somewhere in the Bronx.

No. Too many risks. At least three people had seen him in this car – the patrolman and the two workmen. They might remember. And suppose someone at Seventy-second Street boarded the car while Paul was stepping out of it? A subway was a trap; too easy to be cornered.

If they accosted him he would take the risk. Otherwise he would let them go. *So it's up to you two*. He watched them narrowly.

They didn't pay him much attention. They both looked sleepy – strung out on heroin? In any event they didn't stir until the train scraped into the station. They were on their feet ahead of Paul and he followed them across the platform and up the stairs. Maybe they would stop and jump him here.

They didn't. Out through the turnstiles, through the back door, across the traffic island and the pedestrian crossing to the corner of Seventy-first and Amsterdam. The boys walked south across the street and down the avenue sidewalk and Paul let them go; the precinct station was just around the corner down there and anyhow it was too close to his apartment. He wondered if they could realise how lucky they were.

19

The party was overcrowded in Sam and Adele's small apartment; people stood around in shifting clusters and the place smelled of the rain guests had brought in on their coats. Despite the cold outside, the air conditioners were running at full blast. There were four couples from the office and Paul knew most of the Kreutzers' other friends but there were five or six strangers – a new couple from down the hall who'd recently moved in from Queens, a psychiatrist Adele had met at a party somewhere, a girl who said she was a free-lance magazine writer doing a piece on East Side apartment dwellers, another couple whose identities Paul didn't catch but whom he kept glancing at because the wife had a hard pinched mouth and the husband had the kind of impersonal efficient eyes you associated with police officials and major-generals. The rest were regulars except for a smartly dressed fortyish lady stockbroker whom Paul had met twice at office luncheons and an old college roommate of Sam's who was in town for the weekend on business – it turned out he was the director of marketing research for a packaging firm in Denver. They were all easy to place and easy to dismiss except for the hard-eyed couple.

The talk was loud and blasphemous with forced heartiness, everyone shouting to be heard; they pounded their speeches through the litany of personal questions and world problems, current movies and politics. Sam and Adele prowled the room refilling drinks and making sure people were mixing with one another – they had always been expert hosts; they introduced Paul to the lady stockbroker and later to the girl magazine-writer as if to say "Take your choice," and a few moments later he spotted them doing the same with the ex-roommate from Denver.

The lady stockbroker revealed a new side he hadn't detected during office hours – a knife-edged garrulous militancy for Women's Lib – and he managed to separate himself from her quickly. The girl doing the article on East Side cavedwellers was jittery and afflicted with a tendency to reach too frequently and aggressively for fresh drinks. She smoked steadily with suicidal drags, jetting smoke from her nostrils. Paul found her equally off-putting and drifted into conversation with the Dundees until Adele went around nudging everybody toward the dining table to collect food from the buffet selection she had laid on. There was a confusion of finding places to sit; they sat on the windowsills and the floor and ate with paper plates on their knees.

Sam brought him a fresh drink. "Careful with this stuff – it's got *water* in it. You know what they say about pollution."

Paul waved his thanks with the glass. "Happy anniversary, Sam."

The talk became looser; crowded together the guests dropped confidences with increasing frankness. Gradually the men became more lecherous, the women more amorous, unburdening themselves to one another with hurt I-want-to-be-loved smiles. The girl who wrote magazine articles said to Paul, "You really seem to understand," and reached out for his hand.

He went to the bathroom less because he needed to than because he wanted escape. He wondered how professional spies stood the pressure.

The Kreutzers were the kind who left things to read in the john. There was a new issue of *New York* magazine that trumpeted *The Vigilante: A Psychiatrist's Portrait* and he opened it and sat on the throne reading about himself.

"A righteous man stalks New York. While the rest of us sit by and talk idly of the administration in city hall and the way the city is going to the dogs, one man is doing something about it. Who is he? What has triggered him?

"Everyone has an opinion. To most of the lawyers I questioned, the vigilante is a vicious outlaw no better than the criminals he stalks. One lawyer said to me, 'Remember the trial in *Alice in Wonderland* where the Red Queen says, "Sentence first, verdict afterwards?"' To some cynics – including several police officers I interviewed – he is doing what we are all tempted to do. Deputy Inspector Frank Ochoa, detailed to nail the vigilante, shrugged when I asked him what he thought of the vigilante. 'He's got a wire down somewhere but I don't think he's a raving maniac. Figure it out, look at yourself. What would you do if you knew you'd never be found out? We've had these guys before. They think they're too smart to get caught.' To the liberals the vigilante is a beast of another species, beyond comprehension. To the blacks of Harlem the vigilante is a Ku Klux Klan-style racist (never mind the fact that of his five victims only two have been black). To a thirteen-year-old boy at P.S. 120 the vigilante is a comic-book sort of hero, an adventurer who wants the chase and flies about the city with a flowing cape bringing vengeance upon wrongdoers à la Batman. To a thoughtful elderly grocer in Spanish Harlem the vigilante is a member of an extinct species which died out about 1918. To a beat pat-rolman in the West Village he is a good citizen assisting the Police.

"I talked with Theodore Perrine, the famous forensic psychiatrist, in his office at the Columbia University Medical School. After issuing the usual disclaimer to the effect that a psychiatrist shouldn't be taken seriously when he tries to psychoanalyze a patient he's never even met (Dr. Perrine does not admire such long-distance whimsies as Dr. Ernest Jones's attempt to psychoana-lyze Shakespeare's Hamlet), the shrink who has prob-ably testified in more banner-headline criminal cases than any other psychiatrist in America made this estima-tion of the character of the vigilante:

" 'We live in a death-oriented society. We anticipate the ultimate calamity and many of us are convinced there's no hope of avoiding it. Our world is a world of conscience-stricken nuclear scientists, and young people who've become disabused of the notion that we have simple problems for which there are solutions. Every-one feels personally betrayed by the way things are go-ing – the future is no longer a rational extension of the past; everything's up for grabs, so to speak. We all tend to feel like laboratory animals who know nothing about the science except what we can observe while we're in the process of being vivisected. That's the milieu in which we all have to navigate, and it's hardly sur-prising that some of us resent it so much that we've begun to hurl ourselves against it more and more irration-ally.

" 'There's a large reservoir of aggression in all of us. We hate crime, yet we don't *do* anything about it. We begin to feel that we're not merely decent people, we're so decent that we're immobilized. That's why a man like

170

this captures our imagination so vividly – he's acting out fantasies we've all shared. He's not the only one acting them out, of course – we've all seen how a great many groups who claim to be for or against something find it necessary to take the law into their own hands. Terrorism has become a legitimized political tool. In that respect the only unusual thing about this fellow is that he's doing it as a one-man operation. If it were an organized effort like the Jewish Defence League or the Black Panthers we'd find it far less fascinating. It's the lone-wolf aspect of it that appeals to the American sensibility. One rugged individualist out there battling the forces of evil – it fits right into our mythology, you see. But other than that, this fellow is merely carrying the accepted concept of political terrorism into the criminal arena.' "

"I asked, 'You mean you don't believe this killer is much more insane than the rest of us?'

" 'Insanity is a legal term, not a medical one. But I should think this man is hardly a raving lunatic. Except for the nature of his crimes themselves, there's nothing inherently irrational in his behavior. It could be interpreted as the logical result of a certain series of psychological inputs. For example, suppose he's a combat veteran who's recently returned from Indochina where GI's take it for granted that if someone gives you a hard time you simply kill him with a fragmentation grenade. The occurrence has become so common in Southeast Asia that "fragging" has become a part of our language.'

" 'Are you suggesting he's a Vietnam veteran?' "

" 'No. He may be, but we have no evidence. If he were, it would be easy to see how he might simply be carrying over the system of values he learned over there to the situation he finds here.' "

" 'You said you feel the vigilante is acting out fantasies many of us share. Do you think that means his actions will influence other people to do the same thing?' "

" 'I expect it to, now that they have this man's example.' "

" 'Then you're saying we're all capable of it – it's only a matter of degree.' "

" 'Not at all. It requires a psychopathic personality – the kind that's capable of muting what we think of as the civilized inhibitions. Guilt, anxiety, social rules, the fear of being apprehended.' "

" 'Then he doesn't know right from wrong, is that what you mean? The legal definition of insanity?' "

" 'No. I'm sure he knows right from wrong quite acutely. He's probably more of a moralist and less of a hypocrite than most of us.' "

"Dr. Perrine is a tall man, bald with a white monk's fringe clasping his skull above the ears. He talks with vast lunges and gestures; his hands describe large arcs as he talks. He had a commanding Presence, a great force of personality; it is easy to see why he is in such demand as a witness at dramatic trials. At this point in the interview he pulled his chair over close to me on its casters, leaned forward and tapped me on the knee.

" 'He's less inhibited, that's the controlling factor. He shares that quality with the criminals he assassinates. Most of us have the gut reaction now and then – we see a crime take place, or we hear of one, and we think to ourselves, "I'd have killed the son of a bitch." But we don't kill anyone. We're conditioned against it, and we believe it's wrong to descend to the criminals' level because there has to be a difference between us and them. Look, most of us are all right as long as we don't know

172

the worst for sure. We can pretend. We can stay on the tightrope because we've erected sufficient defences against the hopelessness that inspires this violence in our society. Most of us really don't want to *know* the things that have set this man to killing his fellow men.' "

"Dr. Perrine halved his professional smile; his words fell heavily, dropped like shoes, spaced out, as though he were lecturing to a class of first-year Med students. 'He's a benighted idealist, really; I would judge he's a man who has seen injustice and frustration to an unbearable degree. His experience has made him hate criminals enough to be willing to destroy himself if he can take some of them down with him. It's an *idée fixe*, with him; he's filled with rage and he's found a way to channel his rage into action. He's transfixed by this obsessive hate.

" 'But I see no signs that it's interfered with his capacity to reason. Take for example the fact that all his victims – or all we know about, anyway – have been killed with the same gun. Now guns aren't that difficult to obtain, unfortunately. He could easily have used a different murder weapon each time. He didn't. Why? Because he wants us to know he's out there. It's a message to the city, a warning cry.' "

" 'Like the come-and-get-me phone calls of that mad killer in San Francisco?' "

" 'No. You mean the Zodiac killer. No, I would judge that one is truly psychotic. He's probably pointed a loaded revolver at his own head and found he couldn't pull the trigger; ever since, he's gone around looking for someone who'll do the job for him. No, our man here is not self-destructive – or to be more precise, that's not his primary motivation. What he's trying to do is to alert

173

the rest of us to a danger he believes we aren't suffici-
ently concerned with. He's saying to us it's wrong to
throw up our hands and pretend nothing can be done
about crime in the streets. He believes there *is* something we can do – and he believes he's showing us what
it is.

"'It's rather like the legend of the Emperor's New
Clothes, isn't it. The legend has value only because it in-
cludes one naïve honest child who's frank and uninhibi-
ted enough to announce that the Emperor is wearing no
clothes. As soon as there's no longer a single honest child
to proclaim the truth, the legend loses its meaning.' "

"The smile, this time, is deprecatory. 'I shouldn't like
to give the impression that I regard this man as a brave
valiant saviour holding back crime in the city like a boy
with his finger in the dike. Too many people are beginning to idolize him that way. Actually he's only contri-
buting to the chaotic anarchy of which, God knows, we
have more than enough. In terms of practical effect,
these killings of his are having about as much effect on
the total crime picture as you'd get by administering two
aspirin tablets to a rabid wolf. I hope you'll emphasize
this point in your article. It's no good condoning any
of this man's actions, it's no good trying to put a high
moral tone on them. The man's a murderer.' "

" 'In that connection, doctor, I've heard it said that
the vigilante cares less about seeing people dead than
he cares about watching them dying. The argument goes,
if he really wants justice why doesn't he cruise the streets
with an infra-red camera and take pictures of these
criminals in the act, instead of shooting them dead in
their tracks?' "

" 'I've heard the same thing, even from some of my
own colleagues. But I think that argument misses the

point. This is a man who's been deeply grieved and distressed by some intimate and violent experience. Now if you give a man a universe of pain to live in, he'll do anything he can to get out. I would guess this man has already tried formal justice and found it wanting. He's not concerned with bringing criminals to trial, he's concerned with averting immediate dangers immediately – by removing the miscreants in the most positive and final way possible.' "

" 'You think perhaps he was the victim of a crime and saw the criminal thrown out of court, something like that?' "

" 'Quite possibly, yes. If you know our courts at all you must have seen occasions when a case the prosecution has spent months of agony to build is destroyed by one misguided witness who cuts through all their reasoned legal arguments simply because he doesn't like the colour of the prosecutor's necktie or he had a sister who resembled the defendant's mother. Our legal system is a shambles, we all know that. Punishment, to deter, must be immediate and impartial, and in our courts it is neither. I have a distinct feeling this man knows that firsthand; he's probably been the victim of it.' "

"For a psychiatrist Dr. Perrine seems to have a few unorthodox ideas. I put that to him: 'Isn't it more common for members of your profession to side with the defendants? Crime is a disease to be treated, and all that?' "

" 'I don't subscribe to those old shibboleths. Personally I tend to believe the so-called humanitarian approaches have added greatly to the suffering of society as a whole. We have laws because we need to protect ourselves. To break those laws is to injure society. I long ago gave up believing in the therapeutic approach to

175

crime, except in those cases where you've got a demonstrably curable case of aberrant behavior – certain sex offenses, for example, that are known to be curable by various drug treatments or psychotherapies. But we've gone much too far in the baby-bathwater direction. The function of punishment is not to reform the criminal, it's to protect society by preventing and deterring certain types of misbehavior. The original idea behind putting offenders in jail was simply to get them off the streets and thereby prevent them from committing any more crimes during the period of their punishment. Capital punishment was the same in theory, except of course that its effect was permanent. If I had to hazard a guess I'd say this is our "vigilante's" primary objective – to prevent these people from committing any more crimes. The primary goal of protecting society seems to be what many of us have forgotten in our rush to safeguard the rights of accused persons – and perhaps that's what this man is trying to remind us of.' "

"Dr. Perrine pushed his chair back and stood up. He spoke slowly again, choosing his words; the act of standing up was deliberate, I'm sure, intended to emphasize what he was going to say.

" 'This man has spent his life as a liberal of good conscience. I'm convinced of it. And now he's reacting against many things he's been taught – principal among those things being the idea of tolerance. He's come to realize that tolerance isn't always a virtue – tolerance of evil can be an evil itself. He feels he is at war, and as Edmund Burke put it, "Wars are just to those to whom they are necessary." To this man his private war is the ultimate necessity. Otherwise he wouldn't have started it – he'd have been too frightened. He's a very frightened man.' "

" 'I had the feeling he was just the opposite. You get the impression he has steel cables for nerves.' "

" 'Quite the reverse. He's terrified. It's only that his rage is even greater than his fear.' "

" 'Do you think his fear is real or imaginary?' "

" 'Fear is always real. The question is whether it's justified by the actual conditions. If it isn't you have paranoia in some form.' "

" 'Then he's paranoid?' "

" 'Most of us are, to some degree, certainly if we live in the cities. Usually we get along, we're protected by our neuratic defenses. But sometimes those defenses fail and the ego collapses, and the unconscious terrors burst through into the conscious centers. I'm sure to this man it's a vital and very personal fact, not just a dry statistic, that the heroin addicts in New York outnumber the police by a factor of several thousand to one.' "

" 'Doctor, if you were asked to draw in words a composite psychological portrait of the vigilante, what would you say?' "

" 'It's difficult. So much depends on factors we don't know – his upbringing, his experiences. But I think you can say this much. He's careful, methodical, quite intelligent. Probably an educated man to some degree. Certainly he's not terribly young, I'd say he was at least in his middle thirties and more likely well over forty.' "

" 'What makes you think that?' "

" 'Well it's rather analagous to our emotional reactions to space flights. Those of us in my generation are rather mystified by the whole thing, we don't pretend to comprehend it on the emotional level even though we may understand the scientific basis for it. On the other hand children take it for granted – my younger daughter, for example, has never lived in an age without space flight and television. A little while ago she asked me quite seriously, "Daddy, when you used to listen to the radio, what did you *look* at?" Do you know I couldn't remember? But the point is that the young people have grown up accustomed to shifting circumstances and unstable values. They may not like the things they see happening, they may even act violently to express their idealism, but at bottom they understand and accept the fact that these things do happen. When they act, they act in groups, because that's the dominating ethos. You don't find solitary teen-agers going off into the backwoods to start organic farms; they do it in communes. You don't find individuals protesting the war at the Pentagon – it's always groups, however badly organized. Our youth have become group-oriented; perhaps it's the influence of Marxism. But the rugged individualism, if you want to call it that, which this man stands for, is something our youth have rejected vehemently. And it's also fairly clear that this man is bewildered and hurt by all the drastic things he sees around him – he doesn't understand them, he can't comprehend what's happened let alone accept it. He's fighting back, but he's doing it according to the traditions of *his* generation – not theirs.' "

" 'Then you say you'd draw a picture of a middle-aged man, reasonably well-educated, careful, intelligent. Could you add anything to that?' "

" 'Well I've already said I think he's probably a confused liberal. If he were a right-winger he'd have access to like-minded groups and we'd be more likely to have access to like-minded groups and we'd be more likely to have an entire wave of assassinations – an entire gang of them out there murdering people, rather than one isolated killer. That's the strange thing about rightists, of course, they preach individualism but they're far more adept at organizing themselves than the left. And I'd add that he's probably a man who's alone – really alone – and that this situation is something new and sudden in his life. That is to say, it's quite likely his family was recently taken from him. Killed by criminals, perhaps. That's merely speculation – everything I've said is. But it would explain a number of things, you see. We all know people who seem to lose all their inhibitions the day they get divorced. They do things they wouldn't have dreamed of doing before they were married.' "

" 'You seem convinced the vigilante is a man. Isn't it possible it's a woman?' "

" 'It's less likely, although anything's possible. Women don't resort to overt violence nearly as much as men do. The gun isn't a female weapon.' "

" 'It's been suggested in the press a few times – the fact that the murder weapon is a .32. That's a rather small calibre – they used to call them ladies' pistols.' "

" 'It may also be a practical matter. A small caliber pistol makes far less noise than a .45, you know. But my own impression is that he's a man who's not intimately acquainted with the use of firearms. A small pistol is much easier to handle. Somewhat more accurate, certainly less recoil and noise, and easier to conceal in your pocket of course.' "

"There wasn't much more. But if Dr. Perrine is right – and he has the reputation – then be on the lookout for a middle-aged, middle-class liberal who has just lost his family, possibly to criminal attackers.

"It could be anyone, couldn't it. Someone I know, someone you know. It could be you."

20

He spent the weekend in the apartment except for the Sunday ride to Princeton with Jack. The psychiatrist's pontifications made him uneasy; to what extent were the police guided by his opinions? Would it occur to them to start questioning every middle-aged male whose wife had been the fatal victim of an unsolved crime? How many like him were there?

The gun was the only real clue they could find. It kept coming back to that. He ought to hide it. But he needed it: without it he would be easy prey for any junkie overdue for a fix. Without it he would again have to walk in fear, circumscribing his movements in time and place. It was the only city he knew of in which it was the well-off citizens, the honest people, who were herded into ghettos. Through most of the city you could not walk unarmed at night; through some of it you could not walk unarmed at any time of day.

Take the chance. It was better than the fear.

"I had a call from George Eng," Henry Ives said. He watched as if he were peering into strong light: with his aged head down and his eyes narrowed to slits.

Paul sat forward, forearms resting on knees. He felt the muscles and nerves twitch in his face, worry pulling at his mouth: *I blew it*, he thought, *I fucked up something*.

Ives' smile was without menace but Paul felt a chill. A vein throbbed above Ives' eyebrow, embossed as if by contained anger. Paul pinched his mouth closed with tight compression and breathed deep through his nose.

After a silence that nearly cracked his nerves he heard Ives say in his cool precise voice, "You did a thorough job on the Jainchill matter, Paul. George is deeply grateful. He's on his way to Arizona to close the deal for Amercon. He asked me to pass on to you his congratulations – we all know what a strain you've been under. It takes a great deal of strength to carry on as you have."

Paul straightened in relief; he made an effort to dispose the muscles of his face toward lines indicative of modest appreciation.

"Quite frankly," Ives said, and his eyebrows contracted sternly, "we'd been watching to see how you bore up under it. I can confess now that there were a few who thought it was only a matter of time before you'd be taking three martinis for lunch and letting your work go to pot. Personally I felt you were made of better stuff than that, but I allowed the partners to persuade me to wait and see. I can tell you now you've passed the test with flying colours."

Test? Paul said with uncertain hesitation, "Ye-es?"

"We met this morning in Mr. Gregson's office. I proposed that you be invited to join the firm as a full partner. I'm glad to say the motion was passed unanimously."

Paul pulled his head up in amazement.

Ives' voice dropped almost out of hearing with avuncular confidential smugness. "We all feel you deserve it, Paul." With an effort he lifted himself to his feet and shuffled around the desk, hand outstretched, beaming.

In the night he re-read the *New York* interview with the psychiatrist; he had bought a copy for himself at the stationery store on Seventy-second Street with the same feeling he recalled from boyhood when he'd bought forbidden pulp adventure magazines: the furtive haste, the fumbled coins.

The psychiatrist was uncomfortably close to the truth in his summation. To what extent were the rest of his speculations valid?

What kind of a monster am I?

He studied himself in the mirror. His face seemed haggard; there were unhealthy pouched blisters under his eyes.

"*. . . about as much effect on the total crime picture as you'd get by administering two aspirin tablets to a rabid wolf.*" Well that was wrong. He'd had a staggering effect on the city. It was in all the media. It was the only topic of conversation. Cops were stating publicly that they applauded the vigilante. And in today's *Post*, a story about a Puerto Rican boy – an addict with a lengthy arrest record – found stabbed to death in an alley beside a school in Bedford-Stuyvesant. It added strength to the news item three days ago about a man found murdered by three .22-caliber bullets on East Ninety-seventh Street – a man who had served two terms for armed robbery; he'd been found with an automatic pistol in his pocket. The newspapers were speculating: *Has the vigilante's .32 become too hot to handle – has he traded it in?* But these killings were not Paul's doing; people were getting on the bandwagon.

Have I done enough? It made him think of countless cowboys in countless Westerns who only wanted to hang up their guns.

That was no good. It wasn't a horse-opera with all the bad guys dead in the last reel. *They* were still out there.

182

They would always be out there. You couldn't stop them all. But that was no excuse for giving up. The important thing – the only thing, was knowing you weren't going to give up. Perhaps there were no victors, perhaps there were only survivors; perhaps in the end it would gutter out like the noxious stub of a used-up candle. Perhaps it was all solipsism and none of it mattered to anyone but himself. But what difference did that make?

He called Jack. "Did you talk to them today?"

"Yes. No change. I think we're going to have to learn to live with it, Pop."

"I guess we are."

After he hung up he got into his reversible jacket and picked up his gloves. Touched the gun in his pocket and checked the time – eleven-ten – and left the apartment.

21

From the trees of Central Park he looked across 110th Street at the shoddy stores and tenements. Addicts probably used half of them as shooting galleries.

The cold wind drove right through him; he tucked his face toward his shoulder against it and stared into Harlem. Traffic moved in desultory spurts through the lights.

He moved along inside the park at the edge of the timber. The lights of the taller buildings moved along with him, just beyond the treetops. He stepped out onto Fifth Avenue and crossed northward with the light and began to walk east along 111th Street, across Madison Avenue and on along the dark foul-smelling block to the barricade which the stone-butted elevated track made on Park Avenue. It was like the Berlin Wall, he thought.

He turned north into the ghetto with the solid railway wall to his right and the brooding slum tenements at his left shoulder. He had never been in this area by night; he had only been through it a few times in his life by day, and then only in cars or on the train. It had the air of a foreign city, it didn't have the feel of New York: the buildings were squat and low, there was no bustling traffic, he saw no pedestrians. Not even drunks slept on the steps here; they probably knew it meant sure suicide. It was the antithesis of Times Square and yet the doomed sense of evil was the same. The icy wind made it seem darker; the occasional snowflake drifted on the swaying air; his heels echoed on the pavements and cobblestones

184

and he imagined himself a last survivor searching the streets of a dead abandoned city.

He saw them in silhouette on the rooftop of a four-storey corner tenement: the shifting shadows of a group of people – three or more, he couldn't tell how many. They kept coming over to the edge and canting themselves outward to look downtown. They reminded him of commuters in subway stations leaning out from the platform to see if the lights of the train were coming into the tunnel. That made him realize what these were looking for: the same thing – a train.

He'd heard about this game. A vicious and dangerous one.

He moved close to the wall into the deeper shadows and slipped toward the corner. He stopped before he reached it; stayed out of the pool of corner lamplight, kept to the shadows, fixed his attention on the rooftop beyond the T-intersection. He thought he heard the distant rumbling of the train but perhaps it was only the hum of the city.

He watched them on the rooftop and began to single them out as individuals. Teen-age boys, at least three of them, and there was one girl who appeared at intervals. They seemed to be making trips to and from the roof parapet and he realized they were crossing the roof to pick things up, bringing the things over to the edge and stacking them there.

Ammunition.

Faintly he heard their nasal laughter.

From this low angle they seemed terribly far above him but it was only a real distance of some seventy feet – the width of the street and half the height of the building if you measured it as a right triangle; Paul's line of vision formed the hypotenuse.

185

He had never shot anyone at quite such a long range; he remembered hearing it was difficult to shoot accurately at a steep upward angle. It would have to be done with care.

At least four of them; he had to take that into account too. He felt in his jacket pocket for the spare cartridges and counted them with his fingers – ten. Add to those the five in the cylinder of the revolver. Not much to waste; three shots per target, no more.

He eased closer to the corner and looked around. The spiderwork of a fire escape clung to the side of the opposite building. He thought about that but decided it would be too risky; they could see him if he went to cross the street.

Then he had another idea. He faded back into the shadows and waited.

The train approached. He saw the three boys lift objects in their hands and brace their feet against the low parapet that ran around the edge of the roof. The racket increased and when Paul turned his head he saw the lights of the train rushing along the top of the stone wall. The ground began to shake under him. The train came parallel with him and he saw heads at windows; he swiveled his glance to the rooftop and they were starting to lift and throw their missiles: bricks and chunks of cement, some of them so heavy the boys could hardly lift them and heave. The big ones fell short but there was a thundering rattle of bricks thudding the roof and sides of the train and Paul heard the tinkle of shattered glass. Had it hit someone inside the train?

Another window rattled. A brick bounced off the side of the train and pulverized itself in the middle of the street. The girl on the roof was throwing things too now; Paul counted them carefully and was satisfied there were only the four.

A crash of glass; he was sure he heard an outcry from the last car; then the train had gone, its rumble hanging in its wake.

He looked back at the rooftop and they had disappeared. He moved quickly to the near corner and put his head out just far enough to see the fire escape across the street.

They were coming down. Running down the metal stair from landing to landing. Their laughter was a cruel abrasion.

He let the first of them get to the bottom landing. The boy extended the jump-ladder with his weight, coming down to the pavement as the ladder squeaked rusty resentment. In the uncertain light Paul steadied his aim across his left wrist and as the boy turned to shout up at the others he squeezed the trigger with steady even pressure until the gun went off with a little kick and a squirt of noise and the boy's head snapped to one side under the bullet's impact.

The others saw him fall but didn't know the cause of it and they hurried coming down. Paul waited; there was time, they still didn't know he was there.

They came down and clustered around the prone one and now Paul pumped the trigger and saw it register upon them as one of them dropped with the quick spineless looseness of instant death and Paul's second shot went through the same one and then ripped up a yard of stucco. The third one was wheeling back under the fire escape with amazing quick presence of mind and the girl was diving for a doorway. Paul heard her scream: "Get that mother!" and then the one from under the fire escape was coming after him, running in deadly swift silence with a knife whipping up.

One shot left or two? Sudden terror gripped him and he knew he had to wait, had to make it point-blank because there was no chance for a miss. The boy came straight at him, terrifyingly without sound; Paul had a clear sight of him, the blazing tight expectant eyes, the lips peeled back from the teeth, the wide nostrils flexed like biceps. . . . and then Paul fired and the spinning plug of lead punched a dark disc in the boy's face just below one eye. The boy's scream was a dead cry but he fell against Paul and Paul scrambled back in thundering panic as the falling knife scraped across his wrist; the gun fell to the pavement and skittered away and Paul fell against the wall bent over almost double hugging his stinging wrist: sweat sprang from his face and sucked-in breath hissed through his teeth. The boy rolled and toppled onto his shoulder and Paul pounced on the gun with primitive clear cunning and shot the groaning boy once more in the face.

It was empty now, he knew it, and he swung the cylinder out and punched the empties and dug in his pocket while his eyes scanned the street opposite – the two boys down. *Where was the girl?*

He heard running footsteps somewhere; a door slammed and he winced.

Gone. He stood shaking, snapping the reloaded gun together. Think now.

She couldn't have seen him clearly; he'd never been out in the light. She hadn't seen his face at all; he was sure of it.

The cartridge cases. He'd dumped them out in his fever to reload – but they would have fingerprints on them; he hadn't worn gloves to load the gun. He bent

188

and picked them up and had a hard time finding the fifth one but it was there, in a crack below the lip of the sidewalk, and after he had all five in his pocket he had a look at the boy who had come at him with the knife. The boy was seeping blood into the pavement. This one had come close, seen Paul's face; he had to be dead. Paul shot him in the head.

Even if the other two under the fire escape weren't dead they hadn't got a look at him; it was time to get out of here – what if that girl called the police?

He turned away from the dead boy and walked south, emptied by violence.

He had covered half the length of the block when he looked back and saw the cop standing there.

The cop stood under the light in a frozen attitude but it was plain by the lift of his head that he saw Paul. Paul froze: the gun, forgotten, still dangled in his hand. He knew the cop knew what he was. He waited for the cop to speak, waited for the cop to draw his gun. He had no thoughts of shooting the cop, although he had the gun in his hand; you didn't shoot cops, that wasn't the point of it all.

The cop reached up in the light and took his cap off and held it in his right hand. Then slowly the cop turned his back and stood there without moving.

It took a long while for Paul to absorb what the cop meant by that. Finally his heart began to thud heavily and he turned and walked south to the corner. He looked back and the cop still hadn't moved. He ducked across under the elevated until he had put the barrier wall between himself and the cop, and then he went over to Third Avenue and walked downtown until he found a cruising cab that took him home.

CORONET BOOKS

Loophole

ROBERT POLLOCK

A High-Voltage Blueprint for a Daring Bank Robbery

'Audacious and ingenious. So plausible and true-to-life that its author was actually reported to the CID by a public-minded citizen at the time of a notorious bank robbery'

Evening News

An expert 'peterman' and a redundant architect combine to exploit a *loophole* in a bank's security. The fast moving plot provides a shrewd and fascinating insight into the preparation and execution of a major crime. But one loophole can twist and turn into another!

'A gripping mastery of the techniques and dangers involved'

Times Literary Supplement

CORONET BOOKS

Relentless

BRIAN GARFIELD

**A Gripping Tale of Flight and Pursuit from a
Highly Talented Storyteller**

Five men stole the million-dollar payroll; and their
leader was an ex-Green Beret officer who had been
thrown out of the army for having murdered too many
civilians.

Pursuit flooded around them. But when a savage
blizzard swept the south-west states and all the com-
puterised technology of the FBI was rendered useless,
the burden of capture fell on the shoulders of one man
– a Navajo cop who was forced to use all his Indian
skills in tracking before he ran down the bandits and
exacted retribution.

'A genuine compulsive' *The Observer*

'Very well done' *New York Times*

'Magnificent ... impossible to put down'
The Yorkshire Post

Also published by Coronet Books

FRANCIS CLIFFORD

12505 5	ANOTHER WAY OF DYING	30p
02898 X	HONOUR THE SHRINE	30p
04343 1	THE GREEN FIELDS OF EDEN	30p
17307 6	THE BLIND SIDE	35p
15143 9	ALL MEN ARE LONELY NOW	35p

CLIVE EGLETON

18629 1	SEVEN DAYS TO A KILLING	35p

BRIAN GARFIELD

17873 6	DEEP COVER	50p
18771 9	RELENTLESS	40p

JACK HIGGINS

17852 3	THE IRON TIGER	35p
17853 1	MIDNIGHT NEVER COMES	35p
18297 0	THE SAVAGE DAY	35p
15122 6	NIGHT JUDGEMENT AT SINOS	35p
12774 0	THE KEYS OF HELL	30p

DON SMITH

18625 9	THE PAYOFF	35p
15474 8	THE PADRONE	30p
15685 6	THE MAN WHO PLAYED THIEF	30p

All these books are available at your bookshop or newsagent, or can be ordered direct from the publisher. Just tick the titles you want and fill in the form below.

Coronet Books, P.O. Box 11, Falmouth Cornwall.

Please send cheque or postal order. No currency, and allow the following for postage and packing:

1 book – 10p, 2 books – 15p, 3 books – 20p, 4-5 books – 25p, 6-9 books – 4p per copy, 10-15 books – 2½p per copy, 16-30 books – 2p per copy, over 30 books free within the U.K.

Overseas – please allow 10p for the first book and 5p per copy for each additional book.

Name...

Address..

....